Angela Palumbo

essays by

Laura Andreini
Marco De Michelis
Alberto Bertagna
Sara Marini
Luca Molinari

ON THE ROAD city
Venice

ON THE ROAD
Editor of collection
Laura Andreini

Forma Edizioni srl, Florence, Italy
redazione@formaedizioni.it
www.formaedizioni.it

editorial direction
Laura Andreini

author
Angela Palumbo

editorial staff
Maria Giulia Caliri
Monica Giannini

graphic design and layout
Silvia Agozzino
Isabella Peruzzi
Veronica Paoli

translations
Katy Hannan

photolithography
Forma Edizioni

promotion and marketing
Stefano Baldassarri
Giulia Di Stefano

special projects
Anna Mainoli

external relations
Irene Borsotti

texts by
Laura Andreini
Marco De Michelis
Alberto Bertagna
Sara Marini
Luca Molinari

Angela Palumbo: pp. 30-66, 72-122, 128-156, 160-192, 196-210

* **Angela Palumbo**, architect, graduated in Architectural Project Design in 2021 at the Università della Campania Luigi Vanvitelli. Since 2022, she has worked on doctoral research in Architecture and Cultural Heritage at the same university, collaborating with Professor Luca Molinari. She also works as a freelance architect with several Italian architectural firms. She has written articles for specialised magazines like *Platform Architecture and Design* and *Dromos*, and is also a speaker at Italian and international conferences. In 2023 she attended the Biennale College ASAC – Writing in Residence course, working on the subject of large cities and the absence of large cities in various *Biennali d'Architettura*.

First Edition: July 2025

ISBN 978-88-55211-78-9

Table of contents

Guidebook as a tool

On the Road is a collection of contemporary architecture guidebooks whose purpose is to tell about a place, whether a city or larger area, through its architectural works chosen to be visited and experienced directly.

The guidebook has a convenient special jacket that opens into a map marking the location of the architectural works and interesting sites to visit. On the back are miniature images and addresses of the architectural works described in detail within.

The book starts with short essays explaining the city or area's present day and history and outlining possible future scenarios with planned or imminent projects. Each work features a photograph of the whole, an architectural drawing (plan or section), a short description, and facts including architect, type, year of construction, address, website, and how to visit it.

The finest architecture of each city and suggested routes are represented by this collection of not-to-be-missed, "timeless" buildings that uniquely define their settings. General information and useful tips for travelers help them optimize their visits and quickly understand the essence of the place described.

Museums, theatres, restaurants, hotels and a list of top architectural firms working in the city let visitors turn a regular trip into an opportunity for study or work.

Note: The pinpoints outside the maps at the beginning of the itineraries are viewable on the rear of the book jacket.

Venice

Laura Andreini*

Venice is perhaps the most portrayed city in the world, yet, paradoxically, one of the least understood. Too often seen through the image created for centuries by artists, travellers, writers and tourists, today, we find it hard to understand what it genuinely represents. There is the danger that iconography conceals reality, the postcard beauty blurs the complexity of a dynamic, fragile, urban identity in constant evolution. It is not surprising that we often view Venice as a static city, crystallised in a timeless image. This impression is partly caused by physical expansion restraints that increase the idea of a suspended space, bereft of evolution. And yet, Venice has never truly been stationary. It is an amphibian city, created in a balance between land and water, forming an architectural and urban approach moulded by the environment and by historical, economical and cultural constraints. Although silent and almost indiscernible, its transformations are constant and inevitable, mainly because of its maritime nature.

This guide was created because of the urgent need to erase the idea of a reflected, static and terminated image. It is not limited to describing Venice simply as an object for contemplation, but analyses the city as a complex organism, vulnerable and resilient, and seeks to read the present through its architectural language. This guide to Venice follows a slightly unusual approach in the On the Road series which normally explores cities and transformations through contemporary architecture, concentrating on more recent urban projects. The environmental conditions and space restrictions in Venice make brand new construction difficult, so focus has been placed on existing buildings: a living heritage that continues to provide answers, solutions, and adaptations. Venetian urban identity is not manifested through new iconic architecture, so much as through the materials, the forms, and the ways these aspects are interwoven with water, time, and with the daily existence of those who live and have lived here. Venice is not only a heritage to be preserved, but a system in constant evolution, a living archive in which each transformation leaves legible traces, if one knows where and how to look.

Investigating the city's architectural and environmental dimension means coming to grips with an urban laboratory that has been able to anticipate many of the challenges of our time. Understanding the underlying logic of adaptation by saving space and managing resources, is not only useful for preserving the city, but essential for envisaging new ways of living elsewhere.

The mythical image of Venice is old and worn, almost a cliché. But behind the surface lies a dynamic reality that can and must be reinterpreted. This guide is an invitation to do so: not simply to learn more about a place that is unique, but to seize its potential as a model – or a warning – for cities of the future.

* Laura Andreini is Architect and Associate Professor at DIDA, University of Florence. Co-founder of Studio Archea where she still works, she is also writer and deputy editor for *area* magazine.

Political / geographical facts

country
Italy

language
Italian

area code
+39 041

coordinates
45°26'23"N
12°19'55"E

area
415,9 km²

population
249,466

density
599,82 ab./km²

time zone
UTC+1

city website
comune.venezia.it

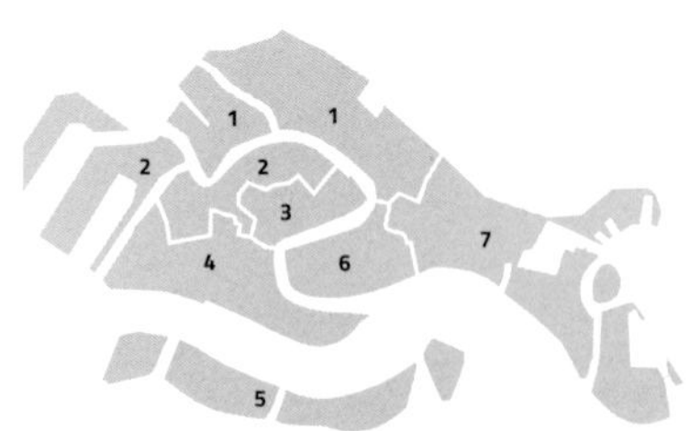

Administrative districts

1. Cannaregio
2. Santa Croce
3. San Polo
4. Dorsoduro
5. Giudecca
6. San Marco
7. Castello

General information
useful addresses and numbers

INFORMATION OFFICES

www.comune.venezia.it/
informazione-e-accoglienza-turistica
Piazza San Marco 71/F

Venezia Unica IAT Piazza San Marco
Piazza San Marco 71/B
Mon - Sun / 9 am - 7 pm

Venezia Piazzale Roma IAT
from the store next to the Agency, Piazzale Roma
Mon - Sun / 7 am - 8 pm

Venezia Unica Stazione FS Santa Lucia IAT
Cannaregio 54/C-D
Mon - Sun / 7.10 am - 9 pm

Marco Polo International Airport (arrivals area)
Mon - Sun / h24

EMERGENCY SERVICES

Emergency telephone number 112

URBAN TRASPORT SERVICES*

Vaporetto (Ferry service / Water bus Service)
The public ferry and water bus services in Venice are run by AVM/ACTV: The water bus service offers a large network of routes through the city canals including connections to the islands of Murano and Burano. Tickets can be purchased from automatic distributors, ticket offices or authorised ACTV retailers. The line most used by visitors is Line 1, which crosses the Grand Canal, stopping at Rialto, Gallerie dell'Accademia, and Saint Mark's.
Hellovenezia +041 24 24 / www.avm.avmspa.it

Water taxis
Taxis stop in public areas at specific jetties called "stazioni comunali taxi" (Municipal Taxi stations).
Radio taxi Venezia 041 59 64

Buses and trams
Travel on the mainland is provided by bus and tram services with the terminal at Piazzale Roma. From this point, visitors can travel around Venice on foot or by ferry and water bus.
App Chat&Go / www.avm.avmspa.it

UNITED STATES CONSULATE
Aeroporto di Venezia Marco Polo,
Viale Galileo Galilei 30
+39 041 5415 944

SPANISH CONSULATE
Corte Amaletea 2646
+39 041 5233 254

HONORARY GERMAN CONSULATE
Palazzo Condulmer, Santa Croce 251
+39 041 5237 675

HONORARY FRENCH CONSULATE
Calle Seconda de la Fava 6140
+39 041 5224 319

HONORARY BELGIAN CONSULATE
Fondamenta Foscarini 3464
+39 041 5242 944

HOW TO PHONE

From a local landline: Just dial the number, including the city code (041)

From a foreign landline: Dial the international code (+39), city code (041) and number

* Ticket categories:
single tickets: € 9.50, valid for 75 minutes (excluding lines 16, 19, Casinò and Alilaguna). Book of 10 tickets (75 minutes each), € 14.00

Useful tips

1. Choosing a hotel in Venice brings you into close contact with its architecture. For a luxury hotel experience, the **Aman Venice** is one of the most captivating. The 16th century Palazzo Papadopoli, on the Grand Canal, is rich in history, frescoes, stucco, and wooden ceilings, revealing the magnificence of Venetian aristocracy. A perfect choice for those who love to be within the architecture, not simply observing it. A more accessible solution is **Ca' Pisani**, a boutique hotel at Dorsoduro, a blend of Rationalist and Déco design. The refined interior appeals to museum and gallery lovers. For those on a tighter budget, try the **Generator Venice** on the Giudecca, an unconventional hostel in a converted industrial building with views of Saint Marks's, a blend of history and young creative spirit.

2. Venice is a city to see on foot or by boat, and naturally, this will influence your travel experience. Those travelling by train arrive at the Santa Lucia Station, close to the historic centre, just a short walk from the Grand Canal. If you prefer to stay on the mainland, Mestre is a good choice with frequent train services to Venice. Buses, water taxis, and the Alilaguna vaporetto all leave from the Marco Polo Airport, perfect for your first impressions of the city. Piazzale Roma is the main terminal for private transport and buses, with access to the internal transport system. Private water taxis will take you directly to your hotel along quiet canals. The internal transport system is the **vaporetti ACTV**, Venice's "floating Metro system", which runs along the Grand Canal and connects all main city zones. Lines 1 and 2 are perfect for admiring the city from the water, with clear views of historical facades. Multi-day tourist tickets provide unlimited travel and are ideal when staying for a few days. It is well worth taking a day to visit the islands of **Murano**, **Burano** and **Torcello**, each with its personal architectural identity and easily reached by vaporetto. Visiting Venice means taking the time to stroll, observe, and lose yourself in wonderful detail: every bridge, *calle* and *fondamenta* has its own story to tell.

3. Venice is also a city of rituals, where age-old celebrations and contemporary initiatives transform public spaces. A visit to Venice during one of these events is a unique experience, where architecture is in close contact with its community. The **Biennale di Venezia** (Venice Biennale) is one of the world's most prestigious art events, dedicated to art, architecture, cinema, dance and theatre. The Architecture Biennale, held every two years (odd years) proposes experimental projects, reflecting on the city, landscape and community. The pavilions in the Giardini and the Arsenale, plus other exhibition sites, show the contrasts between past and present.
Carnival, between January and February, transforms the streets and piazzas, with masked costumes and festivities. The **Festa del Redentore**, the

third weekend of July, celebrates the end of the 1576 plague, with a special Mass; a "votive bridge" of boats connects the Zattere and the Chiesa del Redentore, with firework displays in Saint Mark's Basin.
In September, the **Historic Regatta** recalls the glory of the Venetian navy with parades in Renaissance costumes and regattas with traditional boats. In May, the **Festa della Sensa** celebrates the "Marriage with the Sea", renewing the symbolic bond between Venice and the lagoon. With each event, staged scenery, provisional bridges and backdrops transform public spaces.

4. A five-day stay is ideal for a pleasant visit to Venice, to enjoy the art, architecture, rhythm and flavours of the city. Venice is not a place to visit in a hurry. You should take time to stroll, to discover a hidden courtyard, a quiet bridge, or light reflected on an ancient facade. The day begins in some famous or local café. Try Rosa Salva, for a true Venetian breakfast with some of Venice's favourite pastries: excellent coffee with home-made *fritelle* or *cornetti*. In Cannaregio, Torrefazione Cannaregio serves strong espresso, with the wonderful smell of freshly roasted beans.
A Venetian **tramezzino** sandwich is perfect for a light lunch. Try the Bar alla Toletta, near the Accademia, for tasty combinations like artichokes with tuna, or egg and anchovies. Early in the evening, stop for an aperitif at a *bacare*, traditional inns where they serve **cicchetti** (bite-sized snacks) with **ombra di vino** (a small glass of wine) drinks. The most famous are in Cannaregio and San Polo, but the *bacare* are also common in areas with fewer tourists. Along the Fondamenta della Misericordia, at the Timon, you will find a friendly local atmosphere, with delicious traditional *cicchetti*. At the Arco, near the Rialto Bridge, try the local **baccalà mantecato**, **sarde in saor** and **polpette**. For dinner, many restaurants serve authentic Venetian cuisine. For a traditional but refined meal, try the Antiche Carampane, near the Rialto market, where they serve **bigoli in salsa**, **moeche** and fresh fish dishes. The quiet, tasteful Osteria La Zucca, at Santa Croce, specialises in vegetarian food. Five days in Venice allow you to combine cultural visits while discovering local gastronomy; visit a basilica followed by some shopping in a boutique; see a famous museum, then taste a glass of wine sitting by a canal. In a traffic-free city, where everyone moves on foot or by boat, time seems to stand still. Every corner is an excuse to pause, every aroma is a new discovery.

Modern Venice

Marco De Michelis*

Venice is the result of extraordinary collective intelligence, which was able to transform a vast lagoon into a great city. The early Venetians devised a system to consolidate the lagoon floor by building enormous wooden platforms, shoring up walls for canals, and controlling the waters and sandbars to form a common resource subject to strict regulations. They controlled the rivers that flowed into the lagoon to ensure the regular supply of wood needed to construct the city, its buildings and its ships. The plan drawn up by Cristoforo Sabbadino in 1557, showing the city completely surrounded by "foundations in natural stone", constitutes an amazing document describing the project.

In this way, Venice continued to grow for centuries, conscious of its diversity, until the arrival of the modern era, with its capitalistic production methods, urbanisation, technology and nation states; this was the moment when the very diversity of the city appeared to be a problem, restricting its capacity to adapt to the course of history.

From the 19th century, Venice launched various projects and experiments destined to create industrial areas, the extension of new harbour infrastructures, greater traffic flow expansion, railway lines and essential interchange nodes. Following the construction of the railway bridge in the 1850s which liberated the city from its historic insularity, during the latter part of the 19th century, a series of road connection projects were designed to reach the city centre from the shores of the lagoon. In 1850, Giuseppe Jappelli presented a proposal to extend the railway as far as the shore of the Zattere, which would have housed a large "Entrepôt", then connected to San Marco by an iron suspension bridge. During the same period, projects for the construction of new pedestrian connections and wide straight routes were proposed to connect the railway station with Rialto and the other central areas of the city. Until then, the only bridge crossing the Grand Canal was the ancient Rialto Bridge, so two new bridges were built, one at the Accademia and the other at the Railway station. A fourth bridge, designed by Santiago Calatrava, was built only a few years ago.

During this time, alongside the Arsenale della Repubblica dockyards, which, for centuries, had been a symbol of technological and scientific excellence all over Europe, in the Giudecca, on the Lido, at Sant'Elena and other areas on the outskirts of the urban quarters, new housing projects were built for working class families employed in the new industrial districts, architecturally totally unrelated to the traditional Venetian style of habitation. Between 1905 and 1912, 621 apartments were built for this purpose. A further 289 were built between 1919 and 1921, and construction continued until the 1950s.

The process launched at the end of the 19th century to connect Venice with the mainland was concluded in 1931, finally eliminating the drawbacks associated with the insularity of Venice. It might not have been the last project of this kind, if we remember that in 1959, an urban planning project was

* Marco De Michelis is an architectural historian. He taught at the IUAV University of Venice and was head of the Art and Design Faculty. He has taught and conducted research in many international universities, including Bauhaus-Universität in Weimar and Columbia University in New York. He is the author of cardinal works on modern European architecture and 20th century avant-garde movements.

passed to construct a direct highway route from Mestre, skimming the whole northern side of the historical city centre, to finish on the Lido. Fortunately the project was wisely abandoned in later years. Yet, once again, at the end of the 20th century, a plan was proposed to build an underwater metropolitan train connection between the Tessera airport and San Marco in the heart of Venice. This was submitted as a crucial strategy linked with the proposed universal exhibition planned for the end of the century, but was finally abandoned following fierce opposition.

Despite the fact that Venice had not been badly damaged during the Second World War, in the mid-20th century, it was an impoverished city facing an irreversible economical, political and demographical crisis, which, from 1951, led to a drop in the original residential population from almost 200 thousand, to the 40 thousand residents in Venice today.

The dream of a modern Venice, similar to other contemporary Italian cities, was in striking contrast with its obvious problems, but also with the lack of an efficient strategy that could plan a renewed future for the city. On one hand, Venice was wisely wary of any extremely innovative proposals. In only a few years, the city refused a project by Frank Lloyd Wright who proposed the construction of a small palace/building on the Grand Canal in 1953. Ten years later, the city also refused the plan for a new hospital designed by Le Corbusier, conceived as a strong metaphor of the morphological character of Venice. They also declined a project by the American architect, Louis Kahn, for a new congress centre. The city's near-sighted attitude was dramatically obvious, when we consider its refusal to recognise the outstanding contribution by Venice's leading 20th century architect: Carlo Scarpa.

However, Venice remained a crucial problem for those who attempted to interpret its rationale and particular structure. Once again during the 1950s, Sergio Bettini spoke of the need to produce "an interpretation of visual integrity" that permitted artists an essential freedom of intervention, easily recognisable in the isolated interventions by architects like Samonà, Gardella and, above all, Scarpa. In particular, in a certain manner, the research conducted on urban styles and less important architecture by Ludovico Muratori and Egle Renata Trincanato, paved the way for the works by Aymonino and Rossi at the IUAV university, proposing a morpho-typological interpretation of the Venetian urban style. The aim was to design projects for the city in an attempt to eliminate any discontinuity developed over time, and to re-establish its original urban coherence. In this context, the project designed by Samonà and his colleagues in the international competition for the new Sacca del Tronchetto in 1964, seems truly prophetic: the "Novissime" project envisaged the elimination of all superfluous elements and new buildings constructed in Venice, including the bridges that would connect the historical city centre with the mainland. Reduced to its original basic style, Venice would have been able to reflect once more on its personal identity, respecting the basic objective that Luciano Semerani described as "a reinterpretation of the complex urban structure in certain parts of the city".

This plan did not get started until the 1980s, characterised by a relaunch of the reflections on the future of Venice, also stimulated by the opinion of the city's mayor, Massimo Cacciari, who dared to propose the theory that an audacious transformation was inevitably necessary in order to preserve the city. This led to the first projects which tried to provide modern building solutions coherent with the urban structural style of the city. These included projects by Giancarlo De Carlo at Mazzorbo; the skilful intervention by Gino Valle in the Giudecca (1980-86); the new Saffa area housing project by Vittorio Gregotti; the international competition to design the Campo di Marte in the Giudecca and, a few years later, the competition for the former Junghans industrial area, won by the young Cino Zucchi. The innovative incentive gradually lost its impetus, and petered out at the end of the 1980s. The overwhelming domination of economic questions linked with tourism arose, followed by other problems caused by urgent environmental issues and the protection of Venice from high water damage.

The resulting disaster became rapidly visible. Projects for improving the city were replaced by large-scale looting aimed at multiplying the number of hotel rooms for tourists. The creation of Mose, the mechanical lagoon protection system, concealed the constant deterioration of living conditions in the city. Venice is dying.

From Within, Seagulls Are Not All You See

Alberto Bertagna*, Sara Marini**

An image of the world: within, sublime architecture, its heart formed by its boundaries, enclosed to protect itself, but welcoming the outsider, built and developed, isolating itself while establishing relationships, centrifugal and centripetal, Venice is a collective integer, a mosaic reflected in the floor of the basilica that venerates a smuggled relic, a precise but fragmented identity built from attracting or plundering others; tenaciously desired, devised and constructed; a depository of all things, and within, a noble but brazen postmodernity devoid of truth; an undefinable product of timeless materials and concepts, from elsewhere too, but never defined in number, all perpetually and anonymously, shamefully outsiders, and for this reason, elusive; impossible to determine using non-contradictory principles or linear logic methods.

How does one distinguish between servent and served spaces, primary and secondary elements, (*rii*) channels, (*rii terà*) buried canals like in-ground swimming pools, (*calli*) alleys, (*campielli*) small squares, (*campi*) larger squares, (*fondamenta*) canal side-walks, (*rami*) blind alleys, (*salizade*) paved streets, (*rughe*) shopping streets, (*liste*) restricted lanes, (*corti*) courtyards, (*piazzette, piazzale, piazza*) small, medium or very large squares.

Vehicles are permitted only on the periphery, so squares are always singular, and of course, "Saint Mark's Square" is unique; all streets flow to and from each other, opposite or alongside; the superiority of a salone disdainfully used as a distribution system, lit up by a trifora on a tripartite facade, but always with some detail to interrupt any notion of symmetry, because in Venice, balance is all-important; Pantalone is not only a saint, a church, or a piazza, but is the Carnival mask of Merchant ethics, everything is for sale, perhaps disguised with a gilded layer: "Venice is an *imbroglio*"[1].

But Venice is an imbroglio purely for outsiders; only the uninformed rush into its complexity, far more entangled than its urban layout, a morphological maze that confuses even the toughest taxonomist.

Naturally, even Venice has made mistakes. For a city that based not only its founding principle, but its very existence on its insularity, and which, in its time of maximum splendour distinguished its *dominî da tera* from those *da mar*, the arrival of the railway was more disconcerting than that of Napoleon. Following the railway connection, elsewhere considered as progress, for the first time in its history, Venice became a peninsula and ceased to be the historic location from which all set forth and to which all returned:[2] Saint Mark's Square, whose threshold was marked by the columns of San Marco and San Todaro, doorposts at the entrance of "home".

Although simply an addition to the railway line: the detour destabilised the route and course of events.

Giuseppe Volpi, conte di Misurata, and Vittorio Cini, conte di Monselice, were powerful, staunch Fascists, partners in establishing the CIGA and SADE

* Alberto Bertagna is an architect and associate professor of Architectural and Urban Design at University of Genoa. He is the author of several works: *Dov'è la mia casa?*, *Tic Tac City*, *Il controllo dell'indeterminato*, *La città tragica*, and with Sara Marini, is co-author of *Venice. A Document*, *In teoria*, *The Landscape of Waste*.

** Sara Marini is an architect, and full professor of Architectural and Urban Design at the IUAV University of Venice. She has been the Principal Investigator for the PRIN "Miserabilia" project since 2023, and editor of *Vesper. Journal of Architecture, Arts & Theory* of the Department of Project Cultures since 2019.

companies, launching tourism, and delocalising industry. Years later, in the 1960s, discussions on further expansion of Marghera still continued, although it was clear that it would bring no future advantages, but would lead to even worse problems. It was obvious that the detour had not connected the two worlds, the first: old, tired and with few prospects, and the second in flourishing development. Marghera had attracted and continued to attract its labour force from rural areas rather than from Venice; strikes no longer followed the model of former decades, hungry crowds against Fascist corporatism, but were focussed on a structure already in decline. Everywhere, a challenging new generation was on the rise. In Marghera workers protested strongly against production cycle changes aimed at increasing output. The market was shrinking and factory sirens no longer only signalled work shifts, but warned against vapour leaks creating health hazards. It was blatant that this short-sighted vision brought no economical or social advantages for expansion. During this period, the Venetian workers group was formed, becoming a central element in the united struggles with salaried workers and students in 1967 and 1968, perhaps the only true bridge able to connect Venice with the mainland.

Before the current widespread lack of commitment, at that time, architectural culture was also searching for a solution. With this aim, "Novissime" proposed a "Western front" in Venice to sweep away anything of no specific use, defining two completely opposing points of view.[3]

The Faculty of Architecture in Venice took control, with occupations and demonstrations, uniting workers and students, lagoon and mainland, including the political project action by the Communist Senator, Giuseppe Samonà, to improve not only the urban aspect, but society in general. These years were also marked by strong criticism by Tinto Brass, and perhaps, his character Bonifacio, undecided in his refusal to conform, and instrumental in guiding the destiny of the city.[4]

The final attempt to reach a decision was proposed by Gianni De Michelis, a chemistry professor, and more experienced than others. He understood the repercussions caused by the Marghera disaster, and in his role as Minister of Foreign Affairs, proposed a globalist vision of the city. The idea of hosting Expo 2000 was the last extreme attempt to link Venice with the mainland. But in 1989, Pink Floyd held a concert in the San Marco Basin,[5] and for two days the city was submerged by a mountain of foul-smelling trash that led to cancelling the proposal. The candidacy of Venice was withdrawn in June 1990, only a few days before the decision to be made by the Bureau International des Expositions.

From then on, Venice seemed to watch the exponential increase of outsiders with apathetic indifference, just as Bonifacio participated in social struggles without the passion of Kim, the Marghera worker. In an attempt to create a different future, he was defeated, ending up in a mental hospital, detained on the island of San Servolo.[6]

The islands that once housed mental hospitals are now luxury resorts. Marghera has not yet decided whether to close or expand, even though the Fincantieri dockyard is the only one still afloat. Venice is dying, but not yet, and meanwhile, as it floats on the sea,[7] it markets the performance of its own agony.

Symbol of life, water is both a defence system and a route to the Indies; like death, it moves away[8] when it becomes too suffocating; Mose, the new Redeemer, now repels another plague: the waves of the Adriatic, just as Venice deviated the course of the Brenta, the Piave, and the Sile, and ticket barriers block the waves of tourists. But the railway, highway and airport have not yet prevailed: "Every six hours, tides rise, then fall: the rhythm of the world breathing"[9]. Tomorrow, perhaps an offshore port will break the siege. Meanwhile, from its roof terraces, Venice continues to observe the curious crowds as they arrive.

Here, from its roof terraces, like its seagulls, Venice is always ready to grab any opportunity to try and sustain itself.

1. Francesco Guccini, *Venezia*, in *Metropolis*, 1981.
2. For information on the most famous member of the Milion family, see: Ermanno Orlando, *Le Venezie di Marco Polo*, il Mulino, Bologna, 2024.
3. The group project, led by Samonà, which envisaged the elimination of vehicle access to Venice, and all the recent modern construction development, is well-documented in *Vesper. Rivista di architettura, arti e teoria | Journal of Architecture, Arts & Theory*, no. 1, *Supervenice*, 2019, pp. 170-185.
4. Bonifacio is the leading character in the film by Tinto Brass (1963) *Chi lavora è perduto* who obsessively asks himself whether he should work or not.
5. See Samuel Lorrain, Sara Marini, Léa-Catherine Szacka, *Le concert. Pink Floyd à Venise*, éditions B2, Paris 2017.
6. Another reference to the film by Brass *Chi lavora è perduto* and some of the characters who describe the roots of current Venice through various events in their lives.
7. Francesco Guccini, *Venezia*, cit.
8. "Even if I could, I would not return to live in Venice. It is rotting. These colours come from the putrefaction that has been consuming it for centuries. It is dying. It will return to become the mud it once was". Enrico Maria Salerno, *Anonimo veneziano*, 1970.
9. Carlo Mazzacurati, *La lingua del santo*, 2000.

Venice: Ecosystem Plan

Luca Molinari *

On October 3rd 2020, when the *Mose* was activated for the first time, and high water did not appear in the city, Venetians heaved an unhoped-for sigh of relief. From that day on, the nightmare of the previous year's November floods seemed to have been permanently filed away and Venice confirmed its existence as an amazing artificial landscape whose fragile relationship between land and water is managed through a constant system of social and technological experimentation.

Every urban system can be defined as an unstable landscape of living beings who interact with each other on different levels, contributing towards moulding the physical and immaterial form of the places they inhabit. Venice is one of the most extreme and complex laboratories of this type of situation.

But what is Venice, the city, today? A multi-layered palimpsest of history, monuments and museums that have transformed it into one of the most visited places on earth. A city with two important universities and a student population which has a heavy impact on the overall residential community: less than 48,000 inhabitants in the historical centre, but reaching 300,000 if we include the mainland and the principal islands. These two elements, tourism and university, represent the most important economical and social driving force for a metropolitan system which is facing fundamental strategic challenges to invert its trend towards depopulation and to diversify its particular economical and social system.

Over the next few decades, the vast lagoon system will face certain challenges requiring an essential change in perspective to deal with the problems facing Italy: climate crisis, gradual ageing of the population, and energy and environmental action necessary to renew the existing building stock. In all these spheres, the world of planning design is called to propose decisive ideas and strategies if Venice is to continue to be considered as a living entity, rather than simply a tourist attraction and for a defined period of study.

Within twenty years the Mose protection system will need to be redesigned because water levels continue to rise. This perspective imposes careful consideration of the scale of coexisting landscapes, as well as new technologies necessary for dealing with such radical changes. This involves a more diffused, complex and stratified global panorama demanding immediate research and experimentation in order to be effective within a few decades.

There are at least two coexisting scenarios which, as well as the main environmental question, could transform Venice into an important global case study.

For over a century, historic architectural heritage and its protection has been one the most important fields of action, involving renowned architects, and defining one of the characteristics typical of local expertise. This research and project design work will continue in the future, but must be necessarily accompanied by energy and environmental renewal for the vast amount

* Luca Molinari is an architect, critic and curator, and is full professor of Architectural Theory and Design at the University of Campania Luigi Vanvitelli. He curated the Italian Pavilion at the 2010 Venice Biennale, as well as a large number of exhibitions and museum projects in Italy and abroad. He has written essays on contemporary architecture and is the editorial director of the peer reviewed journal *Platform Architecture and Design*.

of residential housing built between the war and the present time, especially on the mainland.

Planning projects must not be limited only to individual buildings, but considered on an urban scale, re-evaluating most of the surrounding collective spaces and reasoning in terms of a complete ecosystem, not simply limited to technical renovation work. Focus on existing building stock and its use could lead to unblocking the traditional lack of housing for the less affluent members of the population: young couples, singles and students, bringing a social and economic mix into the entire Venetian basin, and not simply to the Mestre area. Alongside this perspective, many underused public buildings in the historic centre could be repurposed for health, education and sport, reinforcing an urban identity that has been weakened under the pressure of aggressive hyper-tourism indifferent to the situation.

The traditional Venetian model of squares, piazzas, and passage courtyards, which have always influenced the slow-paced mobility and local lifestyle quality, should be developed as a specific feature to enhance the existing urban model, rather than sacrificing them for use as spaces for retail and food consumption.

The last challenge would be to galvanise the city to become a widespread services laboratory for culture, higher education, new environmental technologies and the arts, spread throughout the whole lagoon area to counterbalance the prospect of a city that seems exclusively designed for tourist hospitality.

Attracting new investments to strengthen the local university system, together with international private businesses and foundations, would encourage the arrival of a new residential population, and would become an economic driving force for the local population and younger generations. This initiative could also make use of existing building stock in the historic centre, and above all, throughout the entire lagoon which should aim at creating an innovative, expanded, interconnected metropolitan scheme.

The objective is to renew what already exists, integrating, demolishing, and reinventing, without occupying new land and environmental resources, already partly compromised. A virtuous example is the transformation of the Biennale di Venezia, currently underway, aimed at recovering extensive existing building stock for coordination with the institution's traditional activities, to provide even more ambitious, advanced cultural research, conservation, education and experimentation. These challenges focus on the core of the project and on reforming its means and processes, so that Venice can continue to be considered as a laboratory for environmental and social innovation in constant renewal.

Marco Polo Airport
Ca' d'Oro
Fondaco dei Tedeschi
Rialto Bridge
Contarini del Bovolo Staircase
Teatro La Fenice
Basilica of
Santa Maria della Salute

Murano Island
San Michele Cemetery
Saint Mark's Basilica
Ducal Palace
Saint Mark's Square
Biblioteca
Nazionale Marciana
Punta della Dogana

JW Marriott
Resort & Spa
Chiesa del Redentore
Spinsters' Church
Basilica of
Santa Maria della Salute
Contarini del Bovolo Staircase
Fondaco dei Tedeschi

Molino Stucky
Gallerie dell'Accademia
Palazzo Grassi
Church of Santo Stefano
Cassa di Risparmio
(Palazzo Nervi-Scattolin)
Rialto Bridge

Strategies for visiting Venice

Itinerary A | Santa Croce – San Polo – Dorsoduro

This tour takes you from Piazzale Roma to Punta della Dogana, through the contrasts and continuity of Venetian architecture. Piazzale Roma is home to modern buildings like **Hotel Santa Chiara/09** and the **Ponte della Costituzione/10** bridge in Calatrava, as well as Rationalist design like the **Palazzo Rio Novo/06** and the **Law Court office buildings/11**. Cross over the bridge to Dorsoduro, and the landscape opens up to the light and water. The **Squero di San Trovaso/14** preserves traditional craftsmanship, while **Casa Cicogna/15** and **Palazzo Experimental/13** show modern elegance in dialogue with the past. On the Zattere, **Fondazione Vedova/16** by Renzo Piano and **Punta della Dogana/17**, restored by Tadao Ando, demonstrate how restoration can reinvent buildings without sacrificing their history. This tour concludes with two symbolic buildings: the **Santa Maria della Salute/18** and the **Peggy Guggenheim Collection/19**, that combines modern art and the spirit of Baroque design. This tour shows the dynamic side of Venice with its natural blend of history and innovation.

Itinerary B | San Marco – Cannaregio

This tour passes through many layers of Venice, where historic and contemporary buildings coexist in harmony. We begin at the **Ponte dell'Accademia/20**, one of the favourite points on the Grand Canal, moving towards **Palazzo Grassi/21** and **Teatrino/23**, restored by Tadao Ando, in a clever combination of concrete, scale and light. Nearby is **Palazzina Grassi/22**, whose daring contemporary interior was designed by Philippe Starck. The **Fondaco dei Tedeschi/29**, was skilfully restored by OMA, transforming a former commercial building into a "vertical piazza", with a panoramic terrace and views of the city. At Cannaregio, **Ca' d'Oro/30** and **Ca' Vendramin Calergi/31** embody the elegance of Gothic and Renaissance design. The tour continues as far as **former Teatro Italia/34**, a rened converted Liberty building, and the **church of Santa Maria dei Miracoli/35**, with its fine Renaissance poly-chrome marble decoration. The tour ends in the monumental Venice, with **San Zaccaria/38**, **Bridge of Sighs/39**, **Ducal Palace/40** and **Saint Mark's Square/41**, where history and modern architectural precision coexist in harmony.

Itinerary C | Giudecca – Lido – Sacca Sesola

This tour includes three islands, San Giorgio Maggiore, Giudecca and the Lido, with monumental architecture, residential construction and contemporary design. We begin with Isola di San Giorgio, dominated by its Palladian basilica. Alongside, is the **Fondazione Giorgio Cini/46**, now housed in a former monastery, while the **Vatican Chapels/47** propose a contemporary vision of sacred space. The **Teatro Verde/48**, surrounded by nature, completes this experience. On the Giudecca, the **Spinsters' Church/49** marks the entrance to an area of urban transformation. The **apartment buildings in Campo di Marte**, with the **Aymonino/50** and **Siza/51** projects, are prime examples of well-integrated modern design. Next is the Palladian masterpiece, the **Chiesa del Redentore/52**, and the **former Junghans area/53**, transformed by Cino Zucchi as a modem residential quarter. The tour ends on the Lido, at the **Blue Moon beach resort/58**, overlooking the Adriatic, with its airy beach design, and Venice on the horizon. This tour shows another, strongly significant side of Venice: a blend of tradition, transformation, and modern lifestyle.

Itinerary D | Castello

This tour on the eastern side of Venice is charged with culture, experimentation and memory. We begin with the **Monument to the Partisan Woman/59**, a threshold between landscape and history, moving on to the Giardini della Biennale, heart of the international art exhibitions. The **Central Pavilion/68** hosts specific exhibitions, surrounded by the national pavilions, each with its distinct architectural identity. The rear of the Giardini leads to the historic dockyards of the **Arsenale/72**. The **Corderie/71** hosts contemporary art installations in a monumental space that recalls its industrial past. Further north, the **Arsenale Porta Nuova Tower/74**, under renovation, reflects the city's desire to restore sites closed for years. The flexible, hybrid design of the **Harbor Brain Building/75**, shows renovated building potential. The tour finishes at the island of San Pietro di Castello, the ancient religious heart of Venice. The **Basilica of San Pietro/73**, with its leaning bell tower and quiet cloisters, offers a moment of reflection away from the tourist flow. This tour reveals a dynamic Venice, looking to the future beyond its cultural margins.

Itinerary F | Murano – Mazzorbo – Tessera – Mestre

This tour travels beyond the physical and symbolic boundaries of Venice: lesser islands, infrastructures and residential quarters where contemporary architecture interacts with the landscape. It begins with the **San Michele cemetery Expansion/76**, where the modern expansion in sober materials reflects the spirit of place. On **Mazzorbo** island, the **residential complex/77** by Giancarlo De Carlo pays special attention to the local context and its community, integrated in the lagoon landscape. In Mestre, the **M9 Museum/80** by Sauerbruch Hutton is a cultural hub whose contemporary design renews the urban fabric. The **INA-Casa Villaggio San Marco distric/81** quarter is an example of post-war building experimentation, important, but often forgotten. The **Aquae Pavilion/83**, built for Expo 2015, is an example of airy temporary architecture, designed for specific events, but transformable for future purposes. The tour concludes with the **IUAV Construction Sciences Laboratory/82** for architectural research at IUAV university. This final tour shows a Venice spread well beyond the centre, where innovation operates on its margins to leave enduring traces.

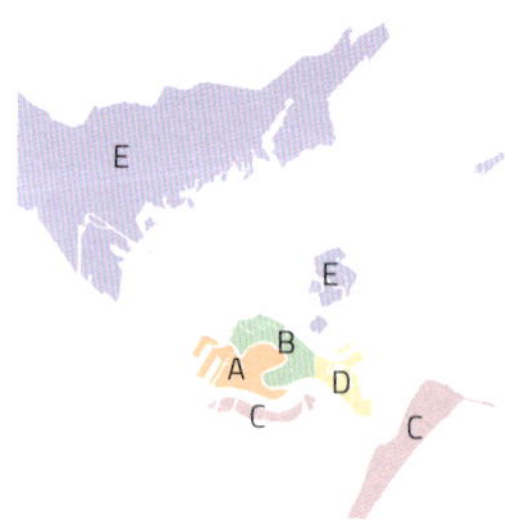

Routes

A. Santa Croce – San Polo – Dorsoduro
B. San Marco – Cannaregio
C. Giudecca – Lido – Sacca Sesola
D. Castello
E. Murano – Mazzorbo – Tessera – Mestre

E

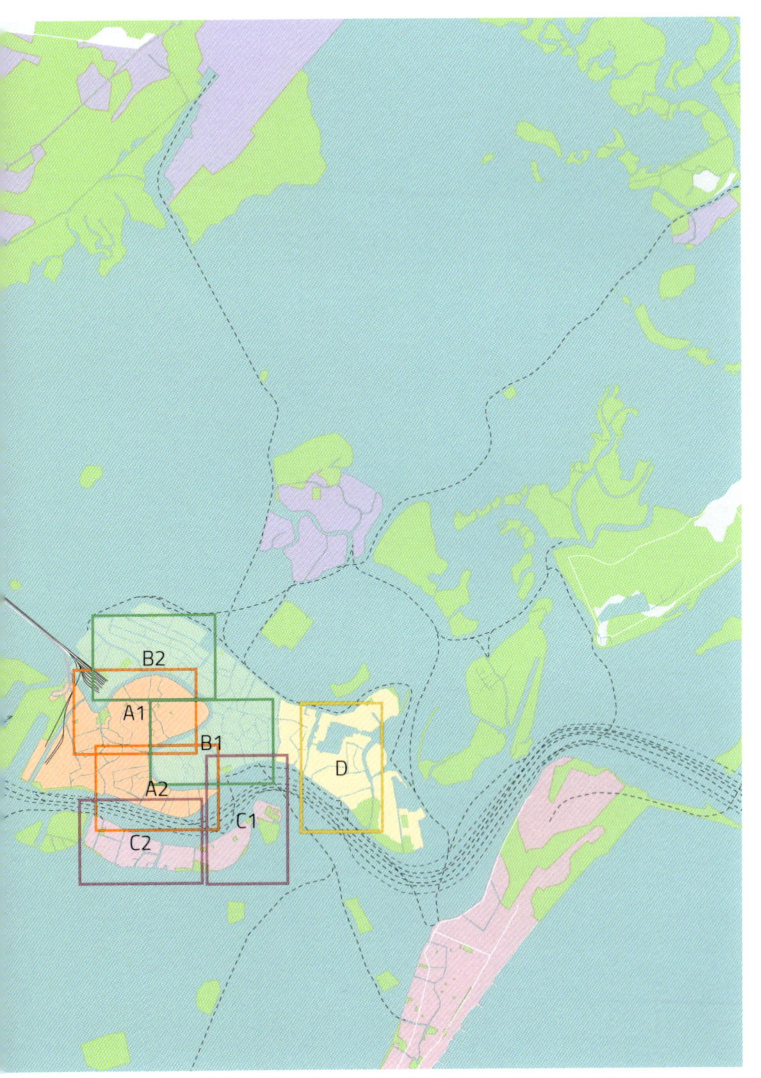
B2
A1
B1
A2
D
C1
C2

F
8
9
Giardino Mistico
Calle de la Misericordia
Rio Terà Lista di Spagna
Stazione di Venezia Santa Lucia
Ponte degli Scalzi
Hotel Canal Grande
Ca' Nigra Lagoon Resort
Palazzetto Foscari
01
Chiesa di San Simeon Piccolo
Ferrovia
Hotel Airone
Calle Sechera
Corte Canal
Zanze XVI
Campo de la Lana
Calle Dario
Calle de la
P.le Roma
10
Ponte della Costituzione
09
Ponte della Libertà
Rio Novo
Giardini Papadopoli
Piazzale Roma
Calle dei Amai
Ostello Domus Civica
Chiesa di San Nicola da Tolentino
08
C. de le Chiovere
Ramo Cimesin
11
Rio Terà Sant'Andrea
Calle Larga Clero
Salizada San Pantalon
Fondamenta de la Fabbrica dei Tabacchi
Calle de la Cereria
Calle Molin
C. Burchielle
Calle Pensieri
Rio Terà dei Pensieri
Rio dei Tre Ponti
Hotel Moresco
Campiello Mosca
Calle Basego
Fondamenta del Rio Novo
06
Fondamenta Rizzi
Fondamenta Procuratie
Calle Contarini
0 m
50 m
200 m
Giorgio Pettenò Architetti
Osteria Alla Bifora

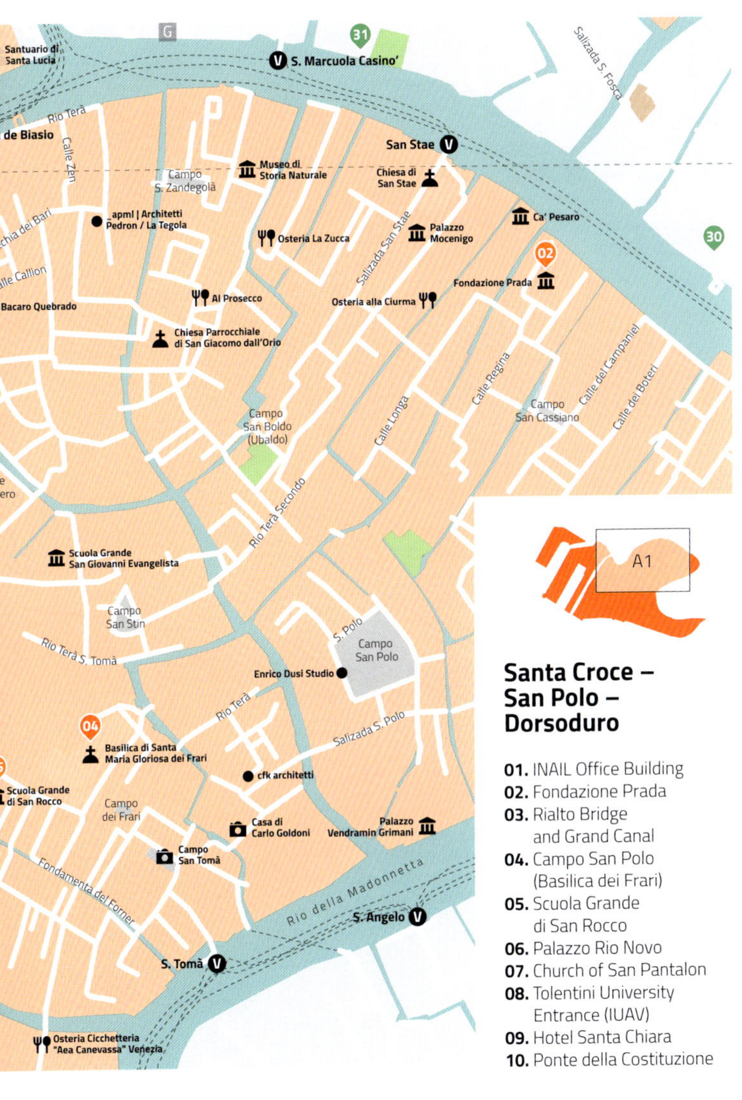

Santa Croce – San Polo – Dorsoduro

01. INAIL Office Building
02. Fondazione Prada
03. Rialto Bridge and Grand Canal
04. Campo San Polo (Basilica dei Frari)
05. Scuola Grande di San Rocco
06. Palazzo Rio Novo
07. Church of San Pantalon
08. Tolentini University Entrance (IUAV)
09. Hotel Santa Chiara
10. Ponte della Costituzione

0 m
50 m
200 m
Calle Contarini
Rio de Ca' Foscari
S. Tomà
Osteria Cicchetteria "Aea Canevassa" Venezia
22
21
Palazzo
Rio Briati
Fondazione Giorgio e Armanda Marchesani
Campo Santa Margherita
Calle de l'Aseo
MAP studio
Osteria Alla Bifora
Osteria Da Codroma
Rio delle Muneghette
Rio Terà Canal
Rio Terà Canal
Calle San Bernardo
C. de le Ca
Scuola Grande dei Carmini
Ca' Rezzonico
9
S. Samue
Studio Zordan
Ponte dei Pugni
Ca' Rezzonico
Hotel Pausania
KANZ Architetti
C. del Tragheto
Calle lunga San Barnaba
Teatro a l'Avogaria
TAMassociati
Calle dei Cerchieri
Calle Avogaria
12
Al Profeta
Osteria Enoteca Ai Artisti
Chiesa di San Sebastiano
Al Vecio Marangon
Rio Terà Ognissanti
Fondamenta Borgo
Accademi
Rio de S. Trovaso
Calle de la Chiesa
Fondamenta Ognisanti
C. dei Frati
Gallerie dell'Accademia
C. del Pistor
C. Cortellotti
C. Larga Nani
Riviera
Rio del Ognissanti
San Basilio
13
14
Hotel Nani Mocenigo Palace
Palazzo Veneziano
Squero di San Trovaso
Palazzo Experimental
Rio Terrà Foscarini
Rio dei Carmini
Osteria Al Squero
Zattere
10
Zattere Gesua
Hilton
Hilton Molino Stucky Venice
55
Fondamenta S. Biagio
F
G

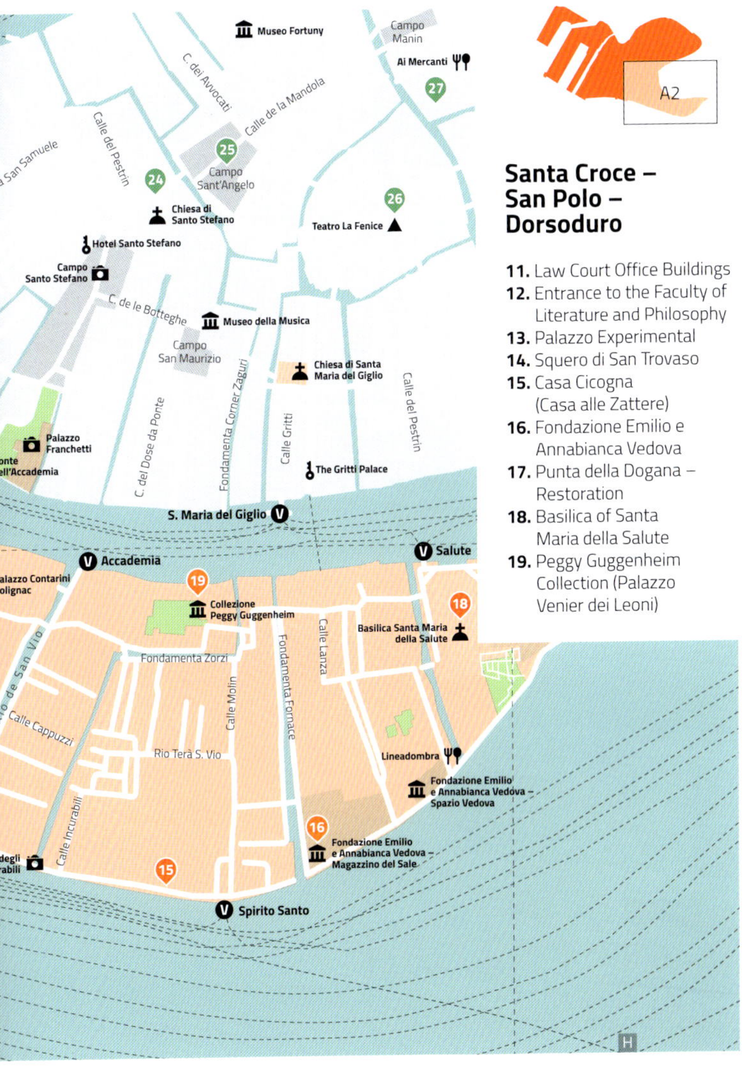

Santa Croce – San Polo – Dorsoduro

11. Law Court Office Buildings
12. Entrance to the Faculty of Literature and Philosophy
13. Palazzo Experimental
14. Squero di San Trovaso
15. Casa Cicogna (Casa alle Zattere)
16. Fondazione Emilio e Annabianca Vedova
17. Punta della Dogana – Restoration
18. Basilica of Santa Maria della Salute
19. Peggy Guggenheim Collection (Palazzo Venier dei Leoni)

01. INAIL Office Building

Sestiere Santa Croce 712,
Corte Nova 706
30135 Venice

external viewing only
+39 041 2729 111

www.inail.it

2, 2/, N > Ferrovia A
1, 2, 5.2, N > Ferrovia B

Designed by Giuseppe Samonà in the 1950s, the INAIL office building is situated in the heart of the Santa Croce sestiere, close to Piazzale Roma. This project represents an important example of Italian Rationalist architecture, in an understated functional style that is discreetly integrated in the Venetian urban fabric without sacrificing its modern design. The building has several floors and is built around a central courtyard that provides uniform natural light and efficient ventilation for the internal spaces. The facade features alternating solid and glazed sections, creating a rhythmic visual sequence that underlines the project's clearly defined configuration. The use of exposed concrete, combined with stone and metal details, provides a solid modern appearance. Great attention was paid to functional design for the interior layout, where administration and office spaces are arranged to optimise user comfort and practicality. This project demonstrates Samonà's capacity to interpret contemporary requirements through an architectural approach that combines practicality with aesthetic sensitivity.

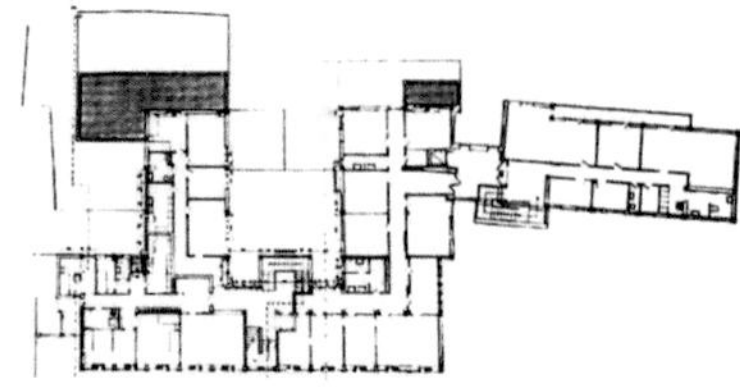

© Petr Šmídek

architects
Giuseppe Samonà,
Egle Renata Trincanato

type
administrative

construction
1952-1960

02. Fondazione Prada

Ca' Corner della Regina, Santa Croce 2215
30135 Venice

May - November
Mon, Wed - Sun / 10 am - 6 pm
+39 041 8109 161
info@fondazioneprada.org
www.fondazioneprada.org

 **1, A, N** > San Stae
1, N > Rialto Mercato

Ca' Corner della Regina, the historic 18th century palace overlooking the Grand Canal, has been the focus of an ambitious restoration project promoted by the Prada Foundation in collaboration with the Fondazione Musei Civici di Venezia. The project was launched with the aim of transforming this historic palace to provide a cultural reference point for the city to host exhibitions, research and activities linked with contemporary art. The restoration work began in 2010, and was carried out in several stages: the protection of architectural and decorative elements, the planning of spaces destined for offices and amenities, and the restoration of the frescoes, stucco, and stone and marble elements. In 2019, a previously hidden fresco was discovered during work on the mezzanine floor. The project also included structural reinforcing and the recovery of the decorative surfaces of the piani nobili. The restoration has now been completed, and Ca' Corner della Regina was reopened to the public in 2023 with a new cultural program that includes exhibitions, conferences and research activities. The palace has become a dynamic cultural centre that makes an active contribution to Venetian art life, preserving and enhancing its rich historical and architectural heritage, and promoting contemporary artistic trends at the same time.

© Marco Cappelletti. Courtesy Fondazione Prada

architects
OMA

type
cultural

construction
18th c.

03. Rialto Bridge and Grand Canal

Ponte di Rialto
30125 Venice

open to the public

1, 2, 2/, N > Rialto
1, N > Rialto Mercato

The Rialto Bridge, one of the most iconic symbols of Venice, is the oldest and most monumental of the four bridges that cross the Grand Canal. Designed by the architect, Antonio da Ponte, and built between 1588 and 1591, it replaced the previous wooden structures in response to the need for a stable and permanent connection between the two sides of the financial and commercial centre of the city. Built entirely of Istria stone, the bridge forms a large, single 28-metre arch, high enough for boats to pass underneath. Its solid structural mass is lightened with porticos and small shops that transform the bridge into an authentic urban space suspended over the water. The bridge rises over the Grand Canal, the backbone of the city and its main communication route. Along the banks of the canal are some of the most important buildings in Venice, testament to the wealth and historic stratification of the Serenissima. Among these are Gothic residences like the Ca' d'Oro, Renaissance palaces like Palazzo Grimani, and others from the Baroque period, like Ca' Rezzonico, in a sequence of different styles that narrate the evolution of Venetian architecture over the centuries. Today, as well as forming the connection between San Marco and San Polo, the Rialto Bridge is one of the most photographed sites in the world and a symbol of Venetian capacity to combine function with timeless architectural beauty.

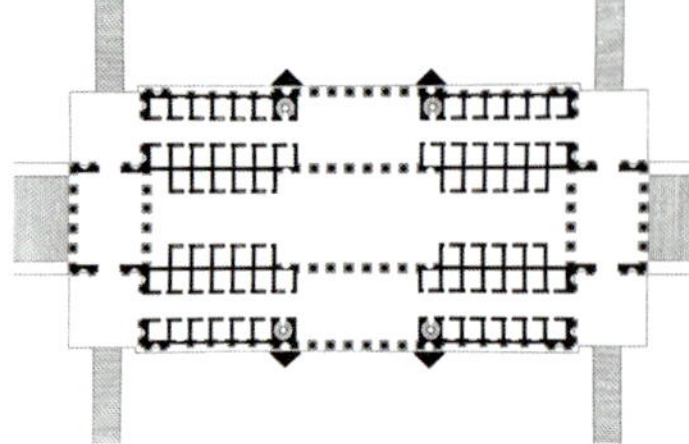

architects
Antonio da Ponte

type
monument

construction
1591

04. Campo San Polo (Basilica dei Frari)

Campo San Polo
30125 Venice

winter timetable
Mon - Sat / 9 am - 6 pm
Sun / 1 pm - 6 pm
summer timetable
Mon - Fri / 9 am - 7.30 pm
Sat / 9 am - 6 pm

www.basilicadeifrari.it

 **1, 2, N** > S. Toma' A, B

Campo San Polo is the second largest square in Venice after Saint Mark's Square. An important urban space, it is renowned for its complex historical and architectural stratification. Originally used to pasture flocks, it was paved over in the 15th century, and for hundreds of years has hosted public events, markets, and celebrations, and still plays an important social role in the community. A short distance away is the Basilica di Santa Maria Gloriosa dei Frari, one of the most important religious buildings in the city. With its imposing mass and brick facade, it represents one of the best examples of the Venetian High Gothic period; the severe but majestic interior is punctuated by slim pillars and pointed arches. The basilica houses several famous Venetian art works, including the monument to Canova, Tintoretto's magnificent mausoleum, and the renowned Assunta, painted by the master himself. The main altar and carved canopy form a masterpiece of beautifully balanced composition that expands the depth of the sacred space. Although serving different functions, Campo San Polo and the Basilica dei Frari represent two fundamental elements in the Venetian way of life: the first, a meeting place and public space for communal activities, and the second, a place of worship and spiritual reflection, symbolising the coexistence of the sacred and the secular in the urban morphology.

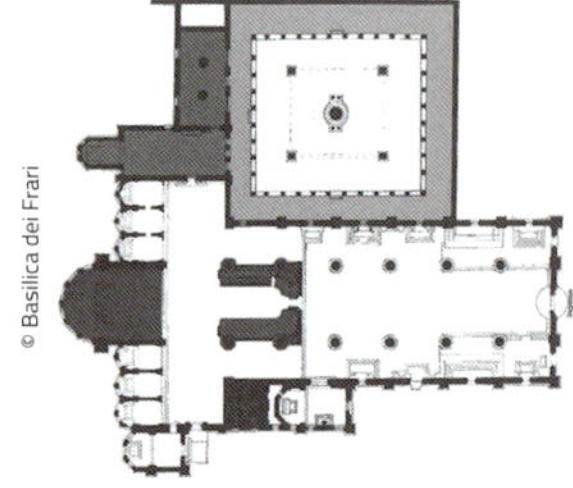

© Basilica dei Frari

architects
Jacopo Celega

type
religious

construction
15th c.

05. Scuola Grande di San Rocco

Campo S. Rocco 3052
30125 Venice

Mon - Sun / 9 am - 5.30 pm
+39 041 5234 864
snrocco@libero.it
www.scuolagrandesanrocco.org

 **1, 2, N** > S. Toma' A, B

The Scuola Grande di San Rocco, located in the San Polo sestiere, is one of the most prestigious lay fraternity schools in Venice. Founded in 1478 and rebuilt after 1517, the school is mainly famous for its cycle of frescoes by Jacopo Tintoretto, one of the finest examples of decorative Mannerism in Europe. The building covers two floors: on the ground floor is the Sala Terrena, an imposing space divided by columns and rounded arches, while the upper floor houses the Sala Capitolare and the Sala dell'Albergo with their magnificent Tintoretto frescoes. The austere, but monumental interior is completely clad in carved gilded wood, enhancing the series of paintings based on episodes from the lives of Christ and Saint Rocco. The external facade, completed in 1549 by Scarpagnino, features an elegant design composed of two orders of rounded Corinthian pillars and gables that create a dynamic effect. The interaction between architecture and paintings reaches its maximum expression in the Sala Capitolare, where the illusionistic perspective of Tintoretto's works amplifies the spatial perception with a unique theatrical impact. Today, the Scuola Grande di San Rocco is a fundamental reference point in understanding the evolution of 16th century Venetian art and the symbiotic bond between architectural design and decorative painting.

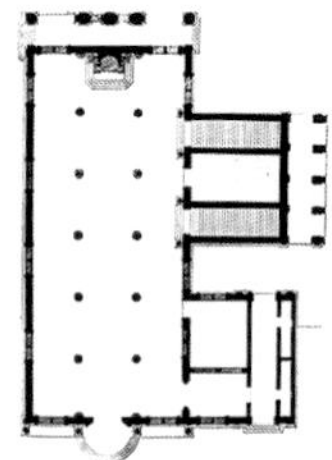

architects
Antonio Abbondi, Pietro Bon,
Sante Lombardo

type
cultural

construction
1517-1560

06. Palazzo Rio Novo

Sestiere Dorsoduro 3488/U
30123 Venice

external viewing only

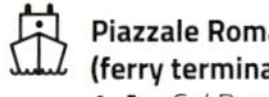

Piazzale Roma (ferry terminal)
1, A > Ca' Rezzonico

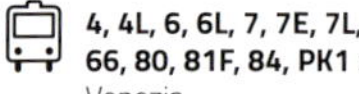

4, 4L, 6, 6L, 7, 7E, 7L, 66, 80, 81F, 84, PK1 > Venezia

T1 > Piazzale Roma

Palazzo Rio Novo, designed by Angelo Scattolin, Cesare Pea and Luigi Vietti in the 1960s, is a striking building set in the centre of Venice, featuring Modernist architecture in communication with the historic urban context. Located in the area near Piazzale Roma, the building has an administrative function and plays a key role in the urban governing of the city. The project is based on the use of simple structures arranged in a strict geometrical composition. The main, stone-clad facade features rows of regular openings, echoing the local monumental style, but subdued by the plain and sober construction details. The use of exposed concrete, combined with glass and metal elements, provides a modern functional appearance. The interior is designed to cater to the operational needs of the public administration, with large, rational open spaces, where natural light plays a fundamental role. Palazzo Rio Novo is an emblematic example of how contemporary architecture can be integrated within a historical context, making a contribution towards modernising the urban image of Venice.

© Petr Šmídek

architects
Angelo Scattolin,
Cesare Pea, Luigi Vietti

type
administrative

construction
1952-1961

07. Church of San Pantalon

Sestiere Dorsoduro 3703
30123 Venice

Mon - Thu, Sat / 10 am - 6 pm
Sun / 9 am - 6 pm
+39 041 2728 611
sanpantalon@gmail.com
www.sanpantalon.it

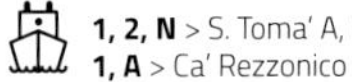
1, 2, N > S. Toma' A, B
1, A > Ca' Rezzonico

The Church of San Pantalon, in the Dorsoduro sestiere, is an important example of Venetian religious architecture, built between the late Renaissance and early Baroque periods. The facade, which remains incomplete, is built in plain exposed brick, in sharp contrast with the richly decorated interior, embellished with one of the most spectacular works of Venetian Baroque art: the ceiling fresco painted by Giovanni Antonio Fumiani between 1680 and 1704. The church has a classical triple nave layout, divided with pillars and pointed arches in a plain sober style to exalt the magnificent sequence of paintings. The 443 square metre ceiling is a triumph of illusionist perspective and theatrical impact, depicting the martyrdom of San Pantalon with an incredible three-dimensional effect that transforms the vaulted ceiling into a space open to the sky. Natural light filters through the side windows, accentuating the depth and movement effects of the composition and exalting the technique of distorted perspective. The main altar in polychrome marble, houses an altarpiece by Paolo Veronese. San Pantalon represents an extraordinary example of a blend of architecture and illusionistic painting; a place where the religious space is transformed to assume an almost dreamlike dimension, a perfect illustration of the theatrical Venetian Baroque style.

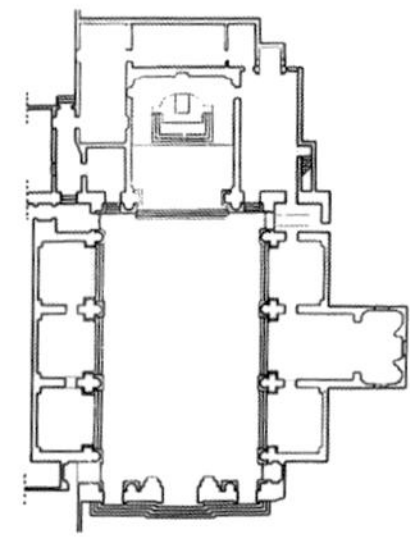

© Алексей Белоусов / flickr.com

architects
–

type
religious

construction
1668-1686

08. Tolentini University Entrance (IUAV)

Sestiere Santa Croce 191
30135 Venice

external viewing only

1, 5.1, 5.2, N >
Riva de Blasio
1, 2, N > S. Toma' A, B

Stazione di Venezia Santa Lucia

T1 > Piazzale Roma

The Tolentini entrance, designed by Carlo Scarpa for the University of Architecture of Venice (IUAV), is a strongly symbolic and extremely refined architectural project. The intervention involves the access to the Tolentini monastery complex which Scarpa transformed, creating a threshold between past and present. The entrance, located on the Rio dei Tolentini, is designed as a sequence of spaces that guide the visitor along a rhythmic route rich in detail. Scarpa used traditional Venetian materials such as marble, bronze and Istrian stone, combining them to create modern, innovative solutions. The central element of the project is the large entrance staircase, designed with steps of varying sizes with beveled edges to create a sense of fluidity. It collects excess high water flow, blending the internal space with the lagoon. Details such as the bronze railings and the play of light on reflecting surfaces reveal Scarpa's outstanding craftsmanship and sensitivity to his materials. The entrance is not simply a functional passageway, but an authentic architectural manifesto: a place of transition that celebrates the interaction between history, nature and modern architecture. This intervention highlights Scarpa's poetic approach, able to transform a simple element like an entrance way into a unique spatial and cultural experience.

architects	**type**	**construction**
Carlo Scarpa	institutional	1985

09. Hotel Santa Chiara

Santa Croce 548
30135 Venice

open to the public
+39 041 5206 955
info@hotelsantachiara.it
www.hotelsantachiara.it

Piazzale Roma (Ferry terminal)

4, 4L, 6, 6L, 7, 7E, 7L, 66, 80, 81F, 84, PK1 > Venezia

T1 > Piazzale Roma

Hotel Santa Chiara, located between the Grand Canal and Piazzale Roma, was designed by the architects Gatto, Lugato and Varratta, and completed in 2016. The project was aimed at integrating modern Venetian design within the logistical and visual complexity of a densely infrastructural area. The project is composed of a well-structured, compact building, whose facade features a rhythmic pattern of alternating ceramic panels and glazed surfaces. Although explicitly contemporary, the materials recall the colour palette of traditional Venetian architecture, creating a dialogue with the historic context, without indulging in contrived imitation. In particular, the use of glass underlines a desire for lightness and transparency, reducing the visual impact of the architectural volume in the urban setting. The project design involved complex challenges including integration with the tourist flow and restrictions concerning historical and urban aesthetics in the area. The open, spacious communal areas connect seamlessly with the exterior, offering exclusive views of the Grand Canal. This project is a specific example of how contemporary architecture can be integrated within an exceptionally complex context such as Venice, demonstrating that ancient and modern are able to coexist by adopting innovative but respectful project design.

architects
Antonio Gatto, Dario Lugato, Maurizio Varratta Architetto

type
hospitality

construction
2016

10. Ponte della Costituzione

Ponte della Constituzione
30135 Venice

open to the public

Piazzale Roma (ferry terminal)

4, 4L, 6, 6L, 7, 7E, 7L, 66, 80, 81F, 84, PK1 > Venezia

T1 > Piazzale Roma

The Ponte della Costituzione, (Constitution Bridge) was designed by Santiago Calatrava and opened in 2008. It connects the Santa Lucia Railway Station to Piazzale Roma, and forms the fourth pedestrian bridge over the Grand Canal. The work is unusual for its contemporary style and the 94 metre steel arch that supports the single span bridge without additional pillars. The combination of steel, glass and Istria stone gives the bridge a modern, lightweight aspect, and reflects the dynamic style typical of Calatrava's work. The glass paving and transparent parapets increase the sense of lightness in harmony with the surrounding landscape. Despite its elegant architecture, the bridge provoked considerable controversy for its costly construction (about 11 million euro) and problems with its maintenance. The glass steps, subject to wear, had to be modified to guarantee safety, and in 2018, a ramp for the disabled was added to increase accessibility. The Ponte della Costituzione is symbolic of the past and future of Venice, a project which, in spite of some criticism, represents an interesting design and cultural challenge for the city.

architects
Santiago Calatrava

type
infrastructure

construction
2008

11. Law Court Office Buildings

Santa Croce 430
30135 Venice

external viewing only

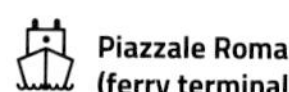

Piazzale Roma (ferry terminal)

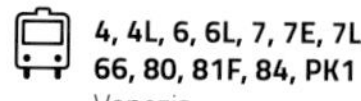

4, 4L, 6, 6L, 7, 7E, 7L, 66, 80, 81F, 84, PK1 > Venezia

T1 > Piazzale Roma
PM > Piazzale Roma

The new Law Court office buildings in Venice, designed by C+S Architects, and completed in 2013, represent an important example of urban renewal in a strategic area of the city: Piazzale Roma. The complex covers an area of over 23,000 square metres, and is part of a very dense infrastructural context in constant transition between the historical city and its main access hub. The project is based on plain austere structures in line with contemporary architecture, focused on functionality as well as its relationship with the surrounding environment. The buildings are located around a central courtyard, in a reinterpretation of the traditional Venetian campiello. This open, light-filled, permeable space creates a balance with the official nature of the legislative offices, with an opening towards the public community. The facade features alternating surfaces in glass, aluminium, and ceramic panels, combining transparent and opaque elements to create a double identity: a symbol of accessible justice, but also discipline and authority. The Law Court office buildings in Piazzale Roma are not simply an example of contemporary public architecture, but are also a fundamental element in the dialogue between the old and new Venice, demonstrating how innovative project design can coexist with and respect the historic and cultural context of the city.

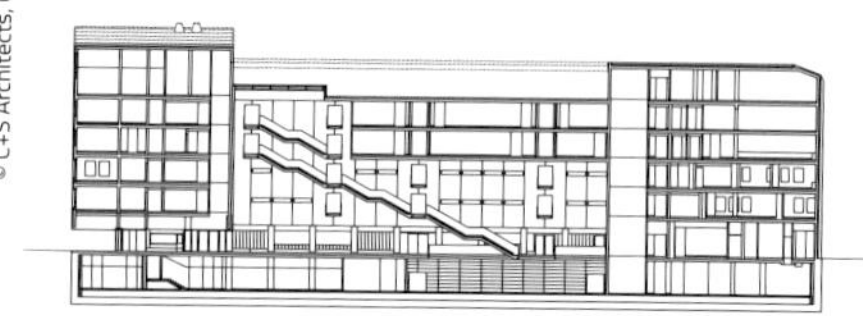

© C+S Architects, Carlo Cappai, Maria Alessandra Segantini

architects
C+S Architects

type
administrative

construction
2013

12. Entrance to the Faculty of Literature and Philosophy

Campazzo S. Sebastian 1686
30123 Venice

open to the public

2, 6, N > San Basilio
2, 5.2, 6, N > Zattere
16, B > Zattere Gesuati
2, 5.1, 6, 10, N > Zattere B

The entrance to the Faculty of Literature and Philosophy in the former Convento dei Tolentini is one of Carlo Scarpa's most refined Venetian projects. Created in the 1970s, the project is a minimal and respectful intervention that has transformed an anonymous space into a passage with great architectural impact. Scarpa designed the entrance as a sequence of cleverly orchestrated elements: steps, ramps and glass panels create a constant interaction between light, materials and routes. His use of Istria stone, concrete and glass reflects his artisanal approach, where every detail is created with meticulous precision. The connection between interior and exterior is designed to create a flow that enhances visual and spatial continuity. The water from the nearby canal, reflected in the glass and other surfaces, becomes an integrated part of the composition, in a poetic reference to the lagoon. This project is an extraordinary example of Scarpa's ability to reinvent existing spaces, bestowing new life and meaning without ever denying their unique historical identity.

© Archipicture

architects
Carlo Scarpa

type
institutional

construction
1976-1979

13. Palazzo Experimental

Fondamenta Zattere
Al Ponte Lungo 1411
30123 Venice

external viewing only
+39 41 0980 200

www.palazzoexperimental.com

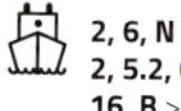

2, 6, N > San Basilio
2, 5.2, 6, N > Zattere
16, B > Zattere Gesuati
2, 5.1, 6, 10, N > Zattere B

Palazzo Experimental, located in the Dorsoduro sestiere, is an excellent example of the restoration of a historic Venetian building for conversion into a boutique hotel. The project, assigned by Experimental Group to the interior designer, Dorothée Meilichzon, was based on careful restoration work and the reorganisation of the internal layout, with a focus on preserving the original elements. The building overlooks one of the city's canals, and its Neoclassical facade was maintained intact, with its regular rows of windows and elegant, sober decorative elements. The communal areas and guest rooms have maintained the traditional Venetian style, with high ceilings, exposed beams, and hand-crafted details that interact with the the plain essential furnishing design. For the cocktail bar design, Meilichzon called on the architect, Cristina Celestino who used refined materials such as marble, wood and velvet in a harmonious palette inspired by the colours of the lagoon, transforming the bar into an intimate welcoming lounge space (clearly visible on the plan and in the photo). One of the most interesting elements of the building is the internal courtyard, transformed into a secret garden, offering an oasis of peace and tranquillity in the dense urban fabric. Palazzo Experimental can be considered as a successful example of a contemporary hotel that enhances the Venetian historic heritage through innovative architectural design.

© Cristina Celestino

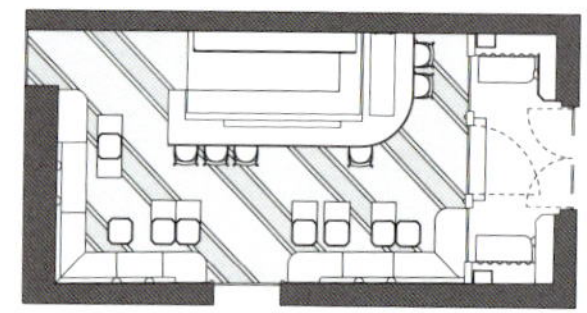

© Cristina Celestino. Photo by Karel Balas

architects
Dorothée Meilichzon
(hotel interior design),
Cristina Celestino
(cocktail bar interior design)

type
multi-purpose

construction
2019

14. Squero di San Trovaso

Dorsoduro 1097
30123 Venice

external viewing only

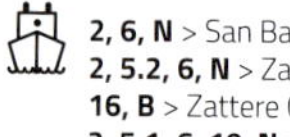

2, 6, N > San Basilio
2, 5.2, 6, N > Zattere
16, B > Zattere Gesuati
2, 5.1, 6, 10, N > Zattere B
1, 2, N > Accademia

The Squero di San Trovaso, situated in the Dorsoduro sestiere, is one of the few boatyards still active in Venice. It bears witness to the historic traditional craftsmanship linked with the construction and maintenance of the city's gondolas. Dating back to the 17th century, the squero stands out for its unusual architecture, reminiscent of traditional mountain chalets of the Cadore region, the original home of many Venetian wood-working craftsmen. The main building, with its wooden structure, pitched roof and large openings, was designed to guarantee maximum functionality for working and drying the wood. The open space in front slopes down gently to the water to facilitate the launching and maintenance of the boats, using traditional methods passed down for generations. As well as being a boat yard, the Squero di San Trovaso is also a symbol of Venetian cultural resilience, a place where one of the city's oldest and most distinctive traditional crafts is kept alive. Its picturesque position in a quiet canal makes it one of the most charming corners in Venice, where time seems to stand still to safeguard an art dating back centuries.

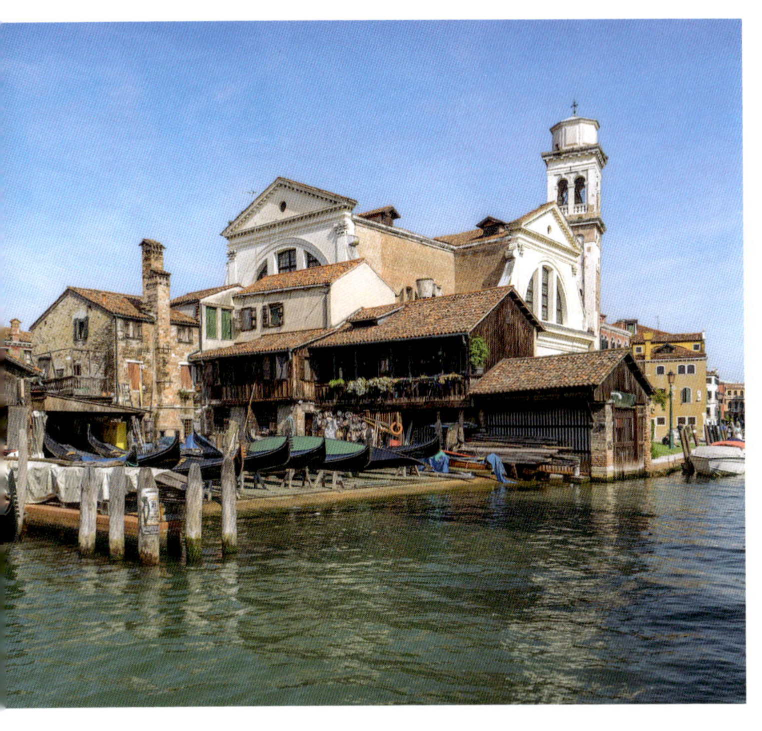

architects	**type**	**construction**
-	commercial	17th c.

15. Casa Cicogna (Casa alle Zattere)

Fondamenta Zattere
Allo Spirito Santo 421
30123 Venice

external viewing only

6 > Spirito Santo
2, 5.2, 6, N > Zattere
16, B > Zattere Gesuati
2, 5.1, 6, 10, N > Zattere B

Casa Cicogna, designed by Ignazio Gardella in 1958, is an exemplary paradigm of modern architecture in Venice, blending harmoniously with its historic surroundings while maintaining its contemporary style. Situated in the Cannaregio sestiere, the building stands out for its sober elegance and perfect integration in the urban fabric. Gardella was able to reinterpret the style of traditional Venetian houses, adapting it to modern requirements, but without eliminating explicit references to tradition. The main facade, in brick and Istria stone, features a strictly regular pattern of windows and arches with Renaissance proportions, but in minimalist style. Inside, the various rooms are arranged around the large centrale drawing room, recalling the typical layout of traditional Venetian homes. However, Gardella introduced innovative solutions like the use of mobile partitions, as well as openings to ensure maximum use of natural light, an essential element in buildings on the lagoon. All materials were chosen with great care to reflect continuity between past and present: Venetian terrazzo flooring, wood and steel detailing, combine with plain modern surfaces. Casa Cicogna is an amazing example of how architecture is able to respect and reinterpret history, without creating an imitation, applying a personal and innovative style in the midst of the Venetian urban landscape.

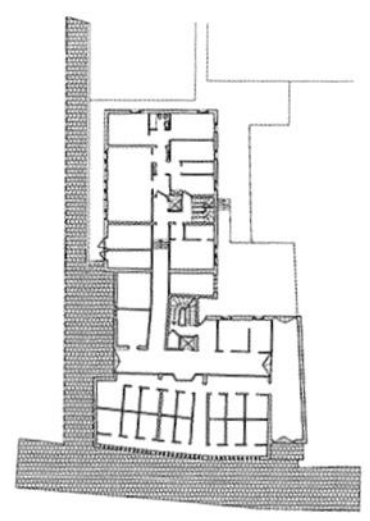

architects
Ignazio Gardella

type
residential

construction
1958-1962

16. Fondazione Emilio e Annabianca Vedova

Dorsoduro 266
30123 Venice

exhibition space
temporarily closed
+39 041 5226 626
info@fondazionevedova.org
www.fondazionevedova.org

6 > Spirito Santo
2, 5.2, 6 > Zattere
16, Alilaguna Blu > Zattere Gesuati
2, 5.1, 6 > Zattere B
1 > Salute

In 2009, the first of the nine Magazzini del Sale (Salt Warehouses), emblematic of Venice's navigational and trading history, was the object of a restoration project by Renzo Piano in collaboration with Alessandro Traldi. The project was commissioned by the Fondazione Emilio e Annabianca Vedova, to transform the ancient warehouse into an innovative and technologically advanced museum space, and to provide a place to show certain works by the artist, Emilio Vedova. The intervention was focused on completely respecting the existing structure, with its long wooden trusses, brick walls and strong support pillars. The architect was able to maintain the monumental effect of the original structure intact, while introducing an avant-garde exhibition element: a suspended metal rail system provides automated handling of the artworks, which are manoeuvred into position in full view of spectators, eliminating the need for partitions or traditional exhibition surfaces. The intervention stands out for the lightweight flexibility of the additions, fundamental in the restoration of such a delicate context. The natural and artificial lighting was designed to enhance the works on display and to accentuate the spatial aspects of the warehouse, highlighting the austere dramatic atmosphere. This design was able to inject new life into a historic building without removing any of its original authenticity, while increasing its expressive and functional capacity.

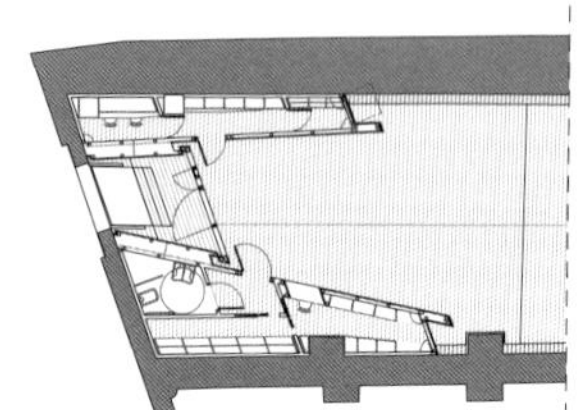

© Atelier Traldi - Alessandro Traldi Architetto
(Atelier Traldi Via Meda 3720141 Milano)

Photo Attilio Maranzano © Fondazione Emilio e Annabianca Vedova, Venezia

architects
Renzo Piano,
Alessandro Traldi

type
cultural

construction
2009

17. Punta della Dogana – Restoration

Dorsoduro 2
30123 Venice

Mon, Wed - Sun /
10 am - 7 pm
+39 041 2401 308
visite@palazzograssi.it
www.pinaultcollection.com/
palazzograssi/it

1 > Salute
6 > Spirito Santo

The restoration of the Punta della Dogana by Tadao Ando and completed in 2009, is a conversion project that combines the conservation of a heritage building with contemporary architectural sensitivity. The former 17th century customs warehouse, situated between the Grand and Giudecca canals, was transformed to create an exhibition space for contemporary art. Ando maintained the original brick and wood structure, leaving its history intact, but meticulously introducing minimal interventions such as exposed concrete walls and steel detailing. The project is based on a flowing itinerary, guiding visitors through a series of dynamic exhibition spaces where natural light enters through the historic openings, modified with modern glazing. Strategic openings provide views of the lagoon, creating constant communication between the interior and the external panorama. The intervention has not only enhanced the historic building, but has created a different interpretation, giving it new life as a symbol of Venetian contemporary design. Punta della Dogana has now been redesigned as a meeting point between art, architecture and history, a prized addition to the context in which it is located.

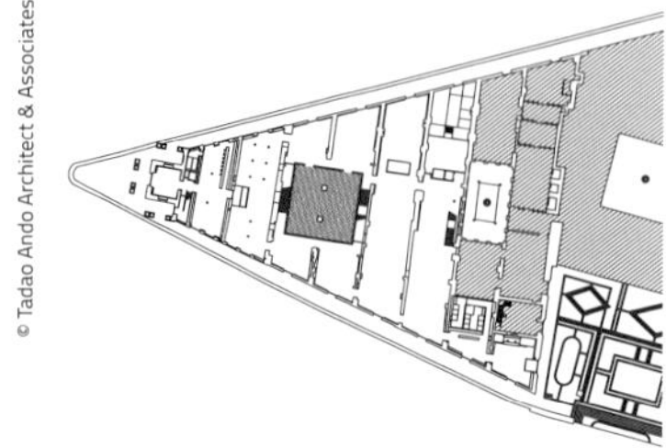

© Tadao Ando Architect & Associates. Photo by Shigeo Ogawa

architects
Tadao Ando
Architect & Associates

type
cultural

construction
2009

18. Basilica of Santa Maria della Salute

Dorsoduro 1
30123 Venice

Mon - Sun / 9 am - 5.30 pm

info@basilicasalutevenezia.it
www.basilicasalutevenezia.it

The basilica of Santa Maria della Salute, the masterpiece created by the architect, Baldassare Longhena, is one of the most iconic buildings of the Venetian Baroque period. The construction began in 1631 to celebrate the end of the plague that had devastated the city. The imposing consecrated basilica dominates the entrance to the Grand Canal; its majestic dome silhouetted against the urban skyline of Venice. Longhena's design is renowned for its central octagonal layout, inspired by Palladian churches, but reinterpreted in a splendid, dynamic style. The spacious interior is emphasised by the light filtered through the large windows, that creates striking contrasts of light and shadow. Above the main altar, also designed by Longhena, is the famous group sculpture of the Vergine della Salute, symbol of the Virgin's protection of the city; the basilica is also home to other famous paintings, including works by Tiziano and Tintoretto. From an urban viewpoint, the church of Santa Maria della Salute represents a visual and symbolic reference point, interacting with the surrounding architecture and creating a harmonious balance with the Punta della Dogana. Every year, on November 21st, the basilica is the focal point of the traditional Festa della Salute, an event that still today, bears witness to the strong bond between the architecture and spirituality of the city of Venice.

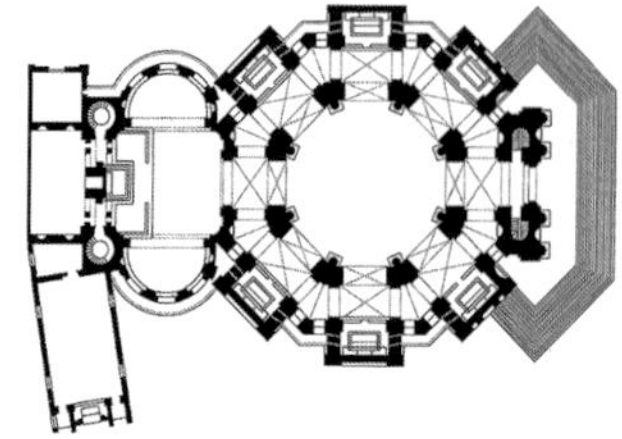

architects
Baldassare Longhena

type
religious

construction
1631-1687

19. Peggy Guggenheim Collection (Palazzo Venier dei Leoni)

Dorsoduro 701
30123 Venice

Mon, Wed - Sun /
10 am - 6 pm
+39 041 2405 411
info@guggenheim-venice.it
www.guggenheim-venice.it

1 > Salute
6 > Spirito Santo

The Peggy Guggenheim Collection, housed in the Palazzo Venier dei Leoni, is one of the most important modern art museums in Italy, and an international reference point for Surrealist, Abstractionist and Abstract Expressionist art. The museum, located on the banks of the Grand Canal, is an 18th century building that had remained incomplete. Peggy Guggenheim, the famous art patron and collector, bought the palace in 1948, converting it to become her residence and a centre to promote 20th century art. Today, the collection exhibits works by Picasso, Kandinsky, Pollock, Miró and Mondrian, offering visitors a voyage through the main artistic currents of the 20th century. The lack of upper floors, caused by the unfinished construction of the building, gives the museum an unusual aspect compared to the surrounding Venetian palaces, creating a fascinating contrast between historic architecture and the modern content of the collection. The collection garden, enriched with sculptures by Giacometti and Henry Moore, forms yet another element which interacts between nature and art. The Peggy Guggenheim Collection is not only a reference point for lovers of modern art, but also a successful example of integrating innovative artistic expression within the historic heritage of Venice.

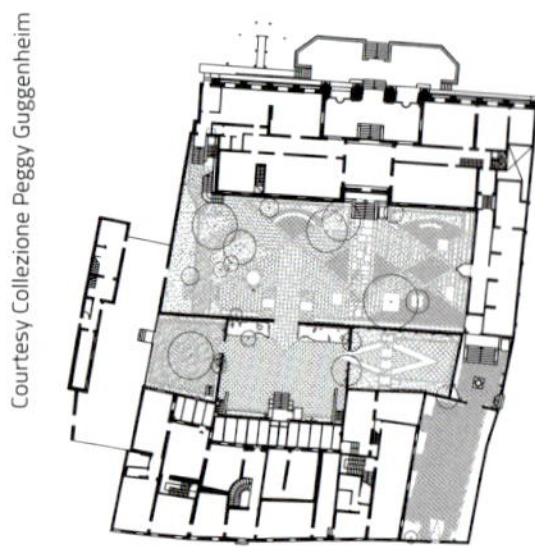

Courtesy Collezione Peggy Guggenheim

© Courtesy Collezione Peggy Guggenheim

architects	**type**	**construction**
Lorenzo Boschetti	cultural	18th c.

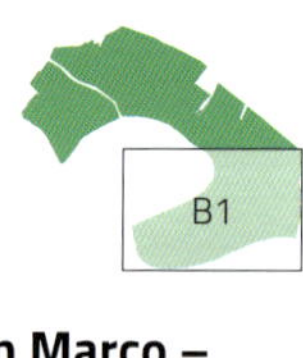

San Marco – Cannaregio

20. Ponte dell'Accademia
21. Palazzo Grassi – Restoration
22. Hotel Palazzina Grassi
23. Teatrino di Palazzo Grassi – Restoration
24. Church of Santo Stefano
25. Campo Sant'Angelo
26. Sala Rossi of the Teatro La Fenice
27. Contarini del Bovolo Staircase
28. Cassa di Risparmio (Palazzo Nervi-Scattolin)
29. Fondaco dei Tedeschi – Restoration
30. Ca' D'Oro
31. Ca' Vendramin Calergi

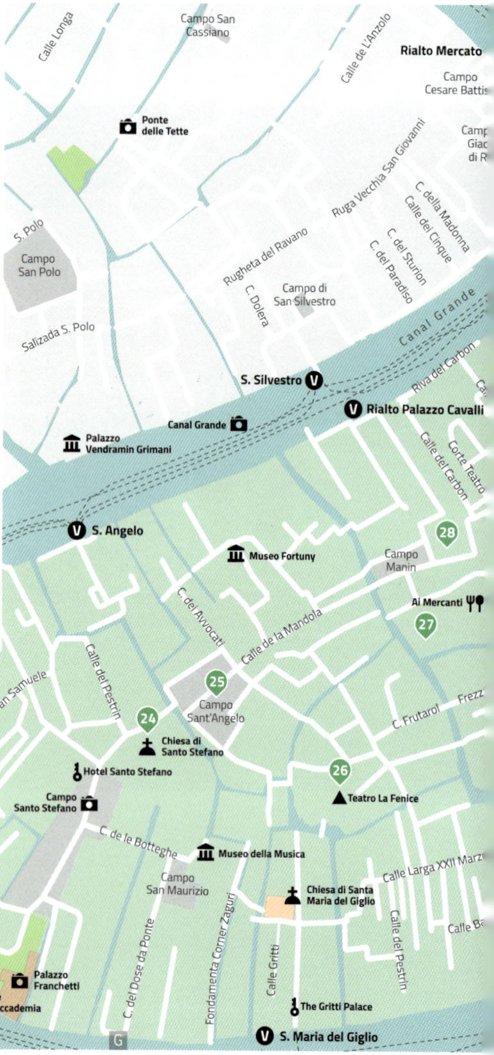

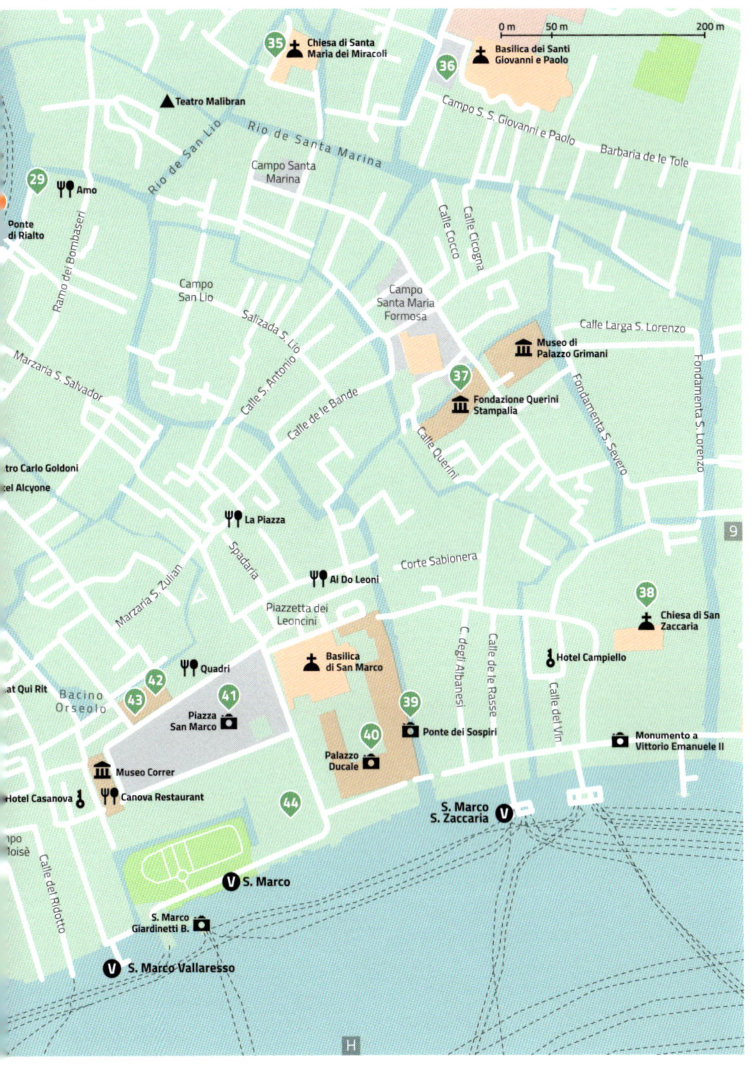

0 m
50 m
200 m
35
Chiesa di Santa Maria dei Miracoli
36
Basilica dei Santi Giovanni e Paolo
Teatro Malibran
Rio de Santa Marina
Rio de San Lio
Campo S. S. Giovanni e Paolo
Barbaria de le Tole
Campo Santa Marina
29
Amo
Ponte di Rialto
Ramo dei Bombaseri
Calle Cocco
Calle Cicogna
Campo San Lio
Campo Santa Maria Formosa
Salizada S. Lio
Calle Larga S. Lorenzo
Museo di Palazzo Grimani
Marzaria S. Salvador
Calle S. Antonio
37
Fondazione Querini Stampalia
Fondamenta S. Severo
Fondamenta S. Lorenzo
Calle de le Bande
Calle Querini
tro Carlo Goldoni
tel Alcyone
La Piazza
9
Spadaria
Corte Sabionera
Al Do Leoni
38
Marzaria S. Zulian
Piazzetta dei Leoncini
Chiesa di San Zaccaria
C. degli Albanesi
Calle de le Rasse
Basilica di San Marco
Hotel Campiello
Quadri
42
at Qui Rit
Bacino Orseolo
43
41
39
Calle del Vin
Piazza San Marco
40
Ponte dei Sospiri
Monumento a Vittorio Emanuele II
Palazzo Ducale
Museo Correr
Hotel Casanova
Canova Restaurant
44
S. Marco S. Zaccaria
mpo
loisè
Calle del Ridotto
S. Marco
S. Marco Giardinetti B.
S. Marco Vallaresso
H

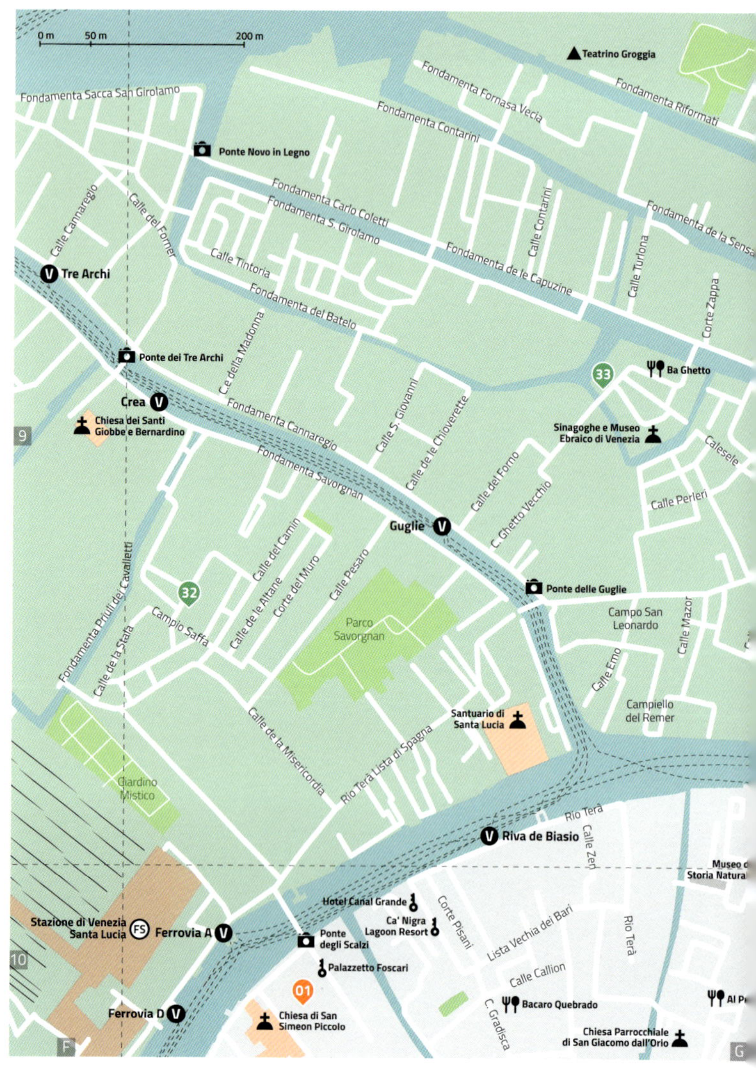

0 m
50 m
200 m
Teatrino Groggia
Fondamenta Sacca San Girolamo
Fondamenta Fornasa Vecia
Fondamenta Riformati
Fondamenta Contarini
Ponte Novo in Legno
Fondamenta Carlo Coletti
Fondamenta S. Girolamo
Calle Cannaregio
Calle del Forner
Calle Contarini
Fondamenta de la Sensa
Calle Tintoria
Fondamenta de le Capuzine
Calle Turlona
Tre Archi
Fondamenta del Batelo
Corte Zappa
C.e della Madonna
Ponte dei Tre Archi
33
Ba Ghetto
Crea
Chiesa dei Santi Giobbe e Bernardino
9
Fondamenta Cannaregio
Calle S. Giovanni
Calle de le Chioverette
Sinagoghe e Museo Ebraico di Venezia
Calesele
Fondamenta Savorgnan
Calle del Forno
C. Ghetto Vecchio
Calle Perleri
Guglie
Calle del Camin
Corte del Muro
Calle Pesaro
Ponte delle Guglie
32
Fondamenta Priuli dei Cavalletti
Calle de le Altane
Campio Saffa
Parco Savorgnan
Campo San Leonardo
Calle Mazor
Calle de la Stala
Calle Emo
Santuario di Santa Lucia
Campiello del Remer
Calle de la Misericordia
Rio Terà Lista di Spagna
Giardino Mistico
Rio Terà
Riva de Biasio
Calle Zen
Museo di Storia Natural
Hotel Canal Grande
Corte Pisani
Ca' Nigra Lagoon Resort
Stazione di Venezia Santa Lucia
FS
Ferrovia A
Ponte degli Scalzi
Rio Terà
Lista Vechia dei Bari
10
Palazzetto Foscari
Calle Callion
01
Bacaro Quebrado
Al P
Ferrovia D
Chiesa di San Simeon Piccolo
C. Gradisca
Chiesa Parrocchiale di San Giacomo dall'Orio
F
G

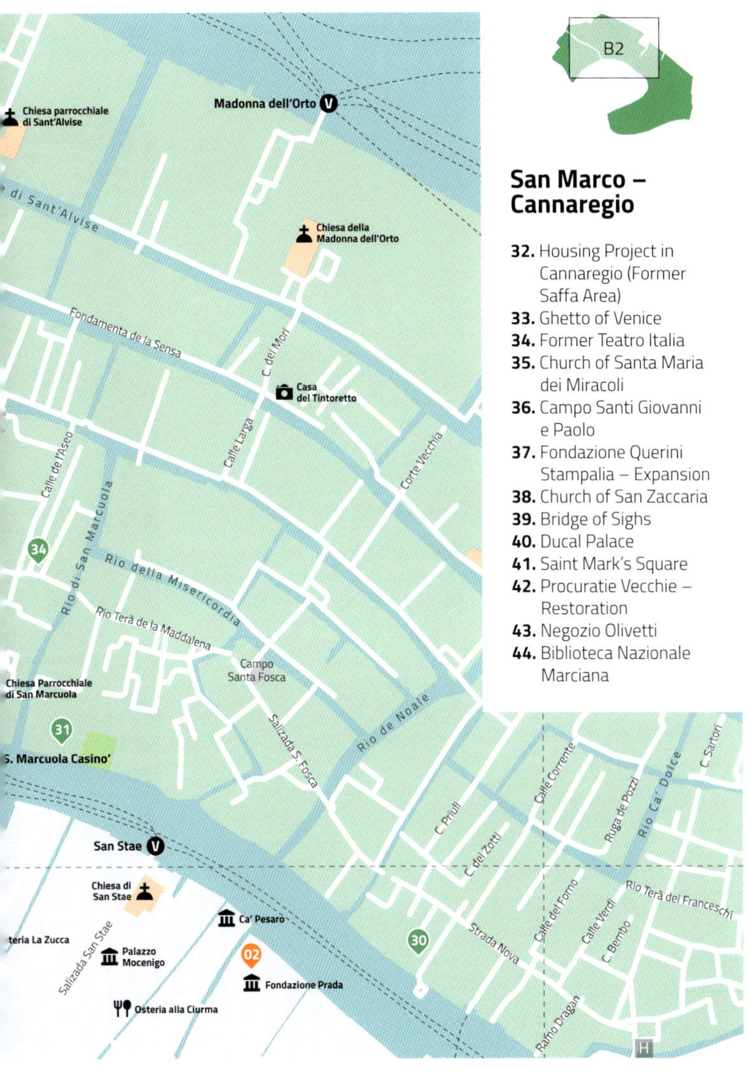

San Marco – Cannaregio

32. Housing Project in Cannaregio (Former Saffa Area)
33. Ghetto of Venice
34. Former Teatro Italia
35. Church of Santa Maria dei Miracoli
36. Campo Santi Giovanni e Paolo
37. Fondazione Querini Stampalia – Expansion
38. Church of San Zaccaria
39. Bridge of Sighs
40. Ducal Palace
41. Saint Mark's Square
42. Procuratie Vecchie – Restoration
43. Negozio Olivetti
44. Biblioteca Nazionale Marciana

20. Ponte dell'Accademia

Campo S. Vidal
30124 Venice

open to the public

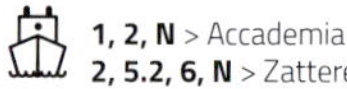
1, 2, N > Accademia
2, 5.2, 6, N > Zattere

The Ponte dell'Accademia, is one of the four bridges that spans the Grand Canal. Its engineering design stands out for its iron and wood structure, an unusual composition in the Venetian context. The present bridge, designed by Eugenio Miozzi, and built in 1933, replaced a previous 19th century iron structure, considered too heavy and lacking in harmony with its surroundings. The bridge has a drop arch structure, with laminated wood trusses that provide a light, continuous effect, consistent with the urban landscape. The choice of wood, an unusual material for bridges of this size, was in response to aesthetic as well as structural needs, to permit a more fluid integration with the surrounding historic buildings. From a functional viewpoint, the bridge connects the banks of the Grand Canal at one of the most important points of artistic interest in the city, linking the Gallerie dell'Accademia with the San Marco sestiere. The panorama from the top of the bridge is one of the most spectacular in Venice, with a privileged view of the Basilica di Santa Maria della Salute. The Ponte dell'Accademia is a virtuous example of engineering applied to a historic context; a modern infrastructure that coexists in harmony with the surrounding ancient urban fabric.

© Daniele Resini. Courtesy Impresa Costruzioni Ing. Enrico Pasqualucci, Impresa Costruzioni e Restauri Salmistrari srl

architects
Eugenio Miozzi

type
infrastructure

construction
1933

21. Palazzo Grassi – Restoration

Campo San Samuele 3231
30124 Venice

Mon, Wed - Sun /
10 am - 7 pm
+39 041 2401 308
visite@palazzograssi.it
www.pinaultcollection.com/palazzograssi/it

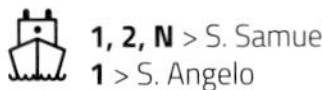
1, 2, N > S. Samuele
1 > S. Angelo

The restoration of Palazzo Grassi, executed by Tadao Ando and completed in 2006, is a magnificent example of how contemporary architecture can coexist with historical heritage buildings. Located on the Grand Canal, the 18th century palace, designed by Giorgio Massari, was converted into a contemporary art exhibition space without modifying its intrinsic character. Ando introduced elements typical of his design style, like polished concrete stairs and ramps, in strong contrast with the richly decorated interior of the original building. The distribution of the internal spaces was redesigned to accommodate the needs of an exhibition space, creating fluid, well-lit environments. Natural light, filtered through the large, restored windows, plays a fundamental role, accentuating the interaction between past and present. The project is especially impressive for its ability to respect and enhance the historical context, with minimal elements that interact with the opulent Venetian architecture. Today, Palazzo Grassi is an iconic space that blends the traditional Venetian Palace with a contemporary vocation dedicated to art and culture.

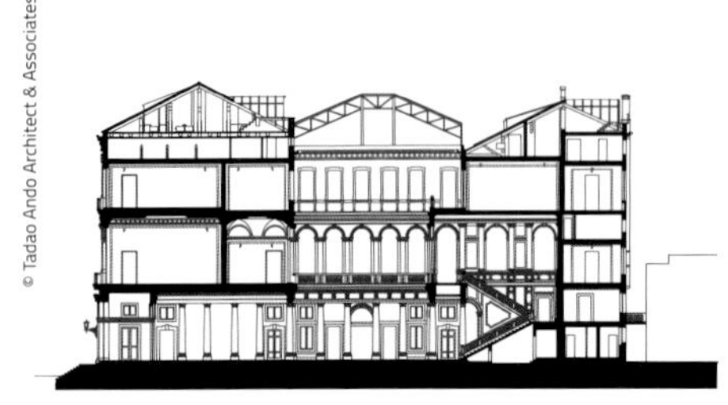

© Shigeo Ogawa. Courtesy Tadao Ando Architect & Associates

architects
Tadao Ando
Architect & Associates

type
cultural

construction
2006

22. Hotel Palazzina Grassi

Ramo Grassi 3247
30124 Venice

open to the public
+39 041 5284 644
info@palazzinagrassi.com
info@palazzinagrassi.com

1, 2, N > S. Samuele
1 > S. Angelo

Hotel Palazzina Grassi, designed by designed by Philippe Starck and H&A Associati, is a boutique hotel that combines contemporary design with the historic fascination of Venice. Situated in a 17th century palace, the hotel offers a new interpretation of Venetian tradition through its modern sophisticated style. The interiors were designed to create a sensuous, intimate atmosphere by skilfully combining materials like marble, glass, wood and precious metals. The communal areas and guest rooms are enhanced with custom-made furnishings to accentuate the comfort and elegance. Lighting has been calculated down to the finest detail, a play of natural and artificial light to create an enchanting environment. Starck's aim was to celebrate the quintessential spirit of Venice using discrete but emblematic decorative touches, like mirrors that reflect fragments of history and current design. Palazzina Grassi represents a perfect balance between nostalgia and innovation, offering a unique immersive experience in the heart of Venice.

Courtesy Palazzina Grassi – Relegance Collection

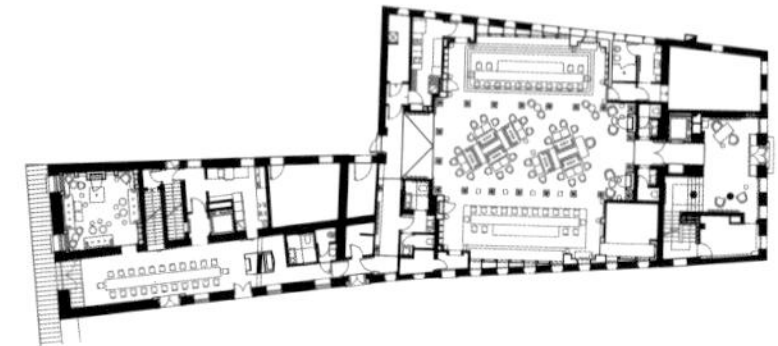

Courtesy Palazzina Grassi – Relegance Collection

architects
H&A Associati,
Philippe Starck

type
residential

construction
2009

23. Teatrino di Palazzo Grassi – Restoration

Campo San Samuele 3231
30124 Venice

Mon, Wed - Sun /
10 am - 7 pm
+39 041 2401 308
teatrino@palazzograssi.it
www.pinaultcollection.com/
palazzograssi/it/teatrino-di-
palazzo-grassi

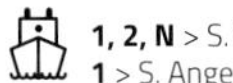

1, 2, N > S. Samuele
1 > S. Angelo

In 2013, the Teatrino di Palazzo Grassi, a small architectural jewel set between the Grand Canal and Campo San Samuele, was given back to the city thanks to a project by the famous Japanese architect, Tadao Ando. Commissioned by the François Pinault cultural holding, the intervention transformed an abandoned space into a cultural hub for performances, conferences and events linked with exhibitions held at Palazzo Grassi. The restoration work maintained the external shell of the building, respecting its integrity and consistency with the surrounding context, but internally, introduced a totally contemporary vision, typical of Ando's style. The structure in exposed concrete, an iconic material, part of the architect's aesthetic, stands out against the dark wood seating and cladding, creating a contrast in texture and colour that enhances the sober elegance of the space. The main auditorium seats 225 spectators and was designed with excellent acoustics and impeccable functionality. Natural light penetrates through sharp geometrical slots in the surfaces, in a play of chiaroscuro with the artificial lighting increasing the impression of volume. The restoration of the small theatre is not limited to a simple architectural renovation project but represents a work that underlines the role of culture in the heart of Venice, combining tradition and innovation through the timeless poetics of Tadao Ando.

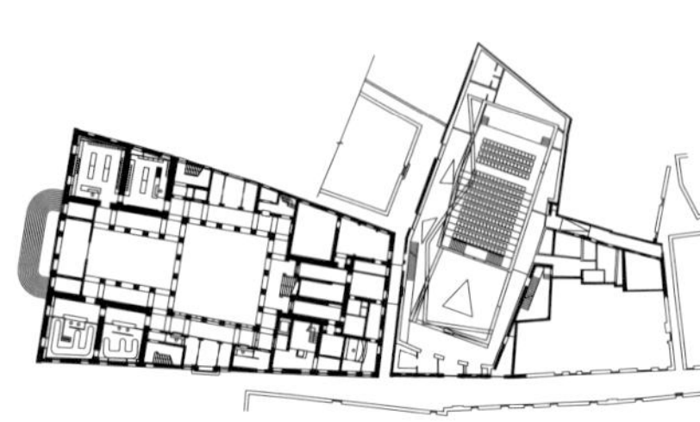

© Shigeo Ogawa. Courtesy Tadao Ando Architect & Associates

architects
Tadao Ando
Architect & Associates

type
cultural

construction
2013

24. Church of Santo Stefano

Campo Santo Stefano
30100 Venice

Mon - Sat / 10.30 am - 5 pm
+39 041 2750 462
info@chorusvenezia.org
www.chorusvenezia.org/visita/chiesa-di-santo-stefano

1, 2, N > S. Samuele
1, A > S. Maria del Giglio

The Church of Santo Stefano, located in the San Marco sestiere, is one of the most important Gothic churches in Venice. Its imposing design shows its strong link with the Order of Augustinian Hermits. The church was first built in the 13th century and extended in the 14th and 15th centuries. It has a single nave layout with an overturned ship's hull roof, a distinctive element of Venetian Gothic churches. The plain simple facade is enriched with a large portal in Flamboyant Gothic style, attributed to the Bon workshop, with three-foil arches and carved decorative elements. The tall spacious interior is divided by large pointed arches that provide the structure with a light airy effect. The polygonal apses and perforated windows enrich the play of light and shadow, emphasising the sense of height. One of the most significant elements of the church is the Renaissance cloister, attributed to Mauro Codussi. It introduces a classical element within a prevalently Gothic context. The marble flooring, side chapels and monumental wooden hull ceiling are outstanding examples of great architectural and decorative quality. The church of Santo Stefano is also an artistic treasure trove with works by Paolo Veneziano, Tintoretto and Bonifacio de' Pitati, which add to the historical and artistic worth of the building.

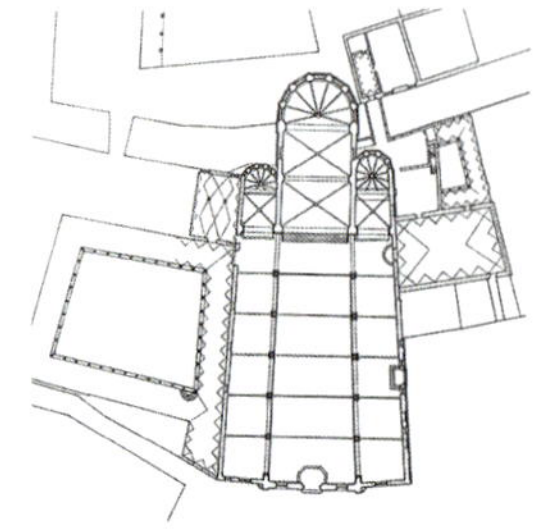

architects	type	construction
-	religious	13th-15th c.

25. Campo Sant'Angelo

Campo Sant'Anzolo
30124 Venice

external viewing only

 **1** > S. Angelo

Located between Saint Mark and l'Accademia, Campo Sant'Angelo is one of the largest public spaces in Venice and represents the meeting point of several historical and cultural circuits in the city; its large open form distinguishes it from other Venetian squares, often smaller and more intimate. The heterogeneous styles of the buildings surrounding the square reflect various stages of evolution in the city: on one side are refined examples of Gothic and Renaissance architecture – like Palazzo Trevisan, with its elegantly perforated facade – and on the other, there are more recent constructions bearing witness to the city's adjustment to evolving necessities. One of the most important examples is a building inspired by 16th century architecture, Palazzo Gritti Morosini, renowned for its sober monumental style and elegantly balanced design. The square takes its name from the historic church of Sant'Angelo, demolished in the 19th century, but whose memory is still alive in the place names of the city. The square has always existed as a place to stroll and meet, and it has remained an active social space over the centuries. Campo Sant'Angelo is still a popular meeting place today; its architectural and urban stratification blends with the daily life of the population, confirming the importance of a public space in Venetian morphology.

architects
-

type
public space

construction
9th-10th c. approx.

26. Sala Rossi of the Teatro La Fenice

Campo S. Fantin 1965
30124 Venice

open to the public
+39 041 786 672
visite@festfenice.com
www.festfenice.com

1, A > S. Maria del Giglio
1 > S. Angelo

The restoration of the Sala Palladio in the Teatro La Fenice, now renamed Sala Rossi, was designed by Aldo Rossi in the 1990s as part of a wider project to renovate and upgrade the theatre. This space, originally planned for secondary purposes, was transformed into a multifunctional concert hall, integrating contemporary necessities without sacrificing the classical and symbolic style for which Rossi was famous. Rossi designed the hall as an interpretation of a classical Italian-style theatre in miniature, with a clever use of materials and geometrical style. The strict, simple layout expresses his vision of an architecture that communicates with history through strongly symbolic design. The walls, clad in wood and precious fabrics, create a warm intimate atmosphere in harmony with the historic colours of the Teatro La Fenice. One unusual element of the project concerns the lighting: the openings and lighting fixtures were specifically designed to enhance the intimate nature of the hall and its multifunctional purpose, creating continuity between past and present. This project is a quintessential example of Aldo Rossi's design method, in which restoration not only concerns conservation, but also the poetic reinterpretation of a space charged with memories.

Mistervlad / Shutterstock.com

architects
Aldo Rossi

type
cultural

construction
1997-2003

27. Contarini del Bovolo Staircase

Scala Contarini del Bovolo 4303
30124 Venice

winter timetable
Mon - Sun / 9.30 am - 5.30 pm
summer timetable
Mon - Sun / 10 am - 6 pm
+39 041 3096 605
cultura@
fondazioneveneziaservizi.it
www.gioiellinascostidivenezia.
it/scala-contarini-del-bovolo/

 **1, 2, 2/, N** > Rialto

The Contarini del Bovolo Staircase, designed by Matteo Raverti at the end of the 15th century, is a masterpiece of Late Gothic Venetian architecture with a certain Renaissance influence that predicted the evolution in style. The most distinctive element of the structure is the spectacular spiral staircase ("bovolo" is "snail" spiral in Venetian), in an elegant cylindrical tower attached to the Contarini del Bovolo Palace. Built of brick with Istria stone inserts, the staircase features a series of superimposed loggias, supported by Renaissance style columns and rounded arches. The double loggia design creates a lightweight, transparent effect, with a refined play of solids and voids that increase the spatial perception. At the top of the staircase is a panoramic Belvedere that provides wonderful views of the roofs of Venice. From a technological viewpoint, the staircase is outstanding for its constructive craftsmanship and for the harmonious blending of the Gothic elements of the Palace facade and the new Renaissance design of the staircase. This intervention represents a rare example of design-based experimentation in Venetian patrician residences, suggesting that the aim was not simply functional, but also for a scenographic and symbolic effect.

© Mattia Micheletto. Courtesy Gioielli Nascosti di Venezia

architects
Matteo Raverti

type
cultural

construction
15th c.

28. Cassa di Risparmio (Palazzo Nervi-Scattolin)

Salizzada S. Luca 4866
30124 Venice

external viewing only

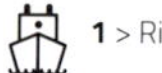
1 > Rialto

The Cassa di Risparmio bank, also known as Palazzo Nervi-Scattolin, was designed in the 1960s by Pier Luigi Nervi and Angelo Scattolin, and represents one of the most daring incursions of Modernism into the Venetian urban fabric. Located close to Campo Manin, the building embodies a combination of technological innovation and respect for the Venetian urban environment. The architectural design is powerful and austere, prominently featuring reinforced concrete, one of Nervi's signature materials. Structural elements like mushroom columns and reticular trusses are an integrated part of the architectural design, a celebration of construction technology and materials. At the same time, Scattolin introduced a sense of restraint and harmony, to ensure that the new building would integrate discreetly within the Venetian context. The interior reflects an explicitly functional layout, with open flowing spaces designed specifically for banking activities, but including refined details such as wood and stone finishes that harmonise with local traditional craftsmanship. This building is an excellent example of Venetian Modernism, able to interpret the essence of the city in a contemporary style without compromising its identity.

© Petr Šmidek

architects
Pier Luigi Nervi,
Angelo Scattolin

type
administrative

construction
1963-1972

29. Fondaco dei Tedeschi – Restoration

Calle del Fontego dei Tedeschi 30100
30124 Venice

1, 2, 2/, N > Rialto

The Fondaco dei Tedeschi, located near the Rialto Bridge, is one of the symbols of Venetian trade architecture. In 1508, it was destined as the main trading post for German merchants, and modified over the centuries. The contemporary restoration, created in 2016 by OMA, led by Rem Koolhaas, with a final execution plan developed by C+S Architects, transformed the building into a multifunctional space integrating modern and traditional elements with refined sensitivity. Constructed around a central courtyard, the building underwent a complete transformation with a glass roof that converted the internal patio into a light-filled atrium. This intervention made it possible to combine the historical appearance with modern-day needs like the creation of a cultural and commercial complex. The internal surfaces highlight the original materials, brick, stone and marble, with the use of modern elements like minimalist stairways and steel railings. Today, the Fondaco is a prime example of how architecture can restore heritage buildings without eliminating the quintessential aspects, making them accessible to a wider, more diversified public. However, the fate of the Fondaco is currently insecure as it is not known if the management company will renew the lease or decide to move it to another building. Yet another opportunity that should not be lost.

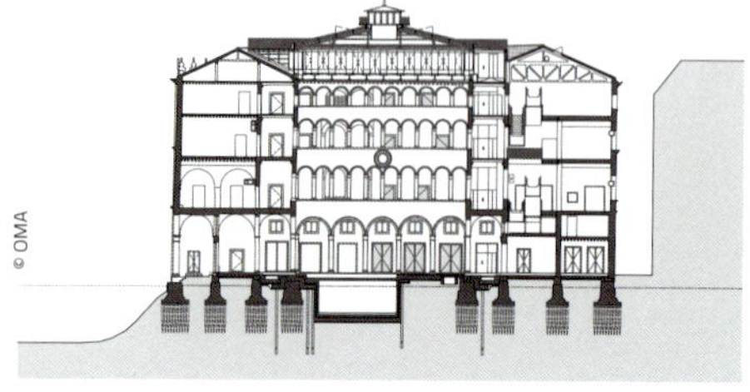

© OMA

Photograph by Delfino Sisto Legnani and Marco Cappelletti, Courtesy OMA

architects
OMA

type
commercial

construction
2016

30. Ca' d'Oro

Ca' d'Oro
30121 Venice

Tue - Sun / 10 am - 7 pm
+39 041 5222 349

www.cadoro.org

 **1, N** > Ca' D'Oro ACTV

Designed by Matteo Raverti and Giovanni and Bartolomeo Bono, built between 1421 and 1434, the Ca' d'Oro is one of the most iconic buildings in Venice. It is considered the peak of Flamboyant Gothic style because of its splendid decorative embellishment and the wonderfully skilled use of Istrian stone. The name originates from the gilded surface that once adorned the facade, giving the building a sumptuous, almost iridescent effect in the sunlight. The ground floor features a portico that opens directly onto the canal, while the upper facade displays a wonderful sequence of three-foil windows and quatrefoil topped columns that intensify the flow between inside and out. The building underwent extensive restoration during the 19th century, transforming it as a museum dedicated to Venetian art. Today, it houses the Giorgio Franchetti Gallery, with works by Mantegna, Tiziano and Carpaccio, as well as sculptures, tapestries, and ceramics of great value. The Ca' d'Oro is not only an extraordinary example of Venetian architecture but also demonstrates how restoration and conversion to museum space can ensure the preservation and fruition of a historic heritage building of incomparable value. On the Grand Canal, the Ca' d'Oro continues to be one of the city's most iconic elements, testament to the glory of 15th century Venice and its role as an artistic and cultural crossroads.

© Tudoran Andrei / Shutterstock.com

architects
Matteo Raverti, Giovanni and Bartolomeo Bono

type
residential

construction
1421-1434

31. Ca' Vendramin Calergi

Campo Seconda del Cristo 2040
30121 Venice

open to the public
+39 041 5297111

www.casinovenezia.it/it/sedi/cavendramincalergi

 **1, 2, N** > S. Marcuola Casino

Designed by Mauro Codussi and completed in 1509, Ca' Vendramin Calergi represents an undeniable example of the transition from the Venetian Gothic to classical Renaissance architecture. Overlooking the Grand Canal, the palace features an elegantly proportioned facade divided into three sections based on the principles of the classical order. Codussi introduced a new Venetian spatial concept, eliminating excessive Gothic decoration in favour of restrained elegance; he focussed on the use of pillars, cornices and gables to define facades with strict geometrical logic. The distinctive element of the facade is the overlapping of serliane, (Venetian windows) a Palladian style architectural element which creates a play of voids and solids that lighten the visual impact of the building. The entrance atrium, typical of Venetian residences, connects the waterfront entry with the internal courtyard, acting as a distribution access and leading to the upper floors decorated with frescoes and refined stucco work. The palace currently houses the Venice Casino, and the building represents a fine example of Venetian architecture and its ability to combine functional and monumental design in a beautifully balanced, refined manner.

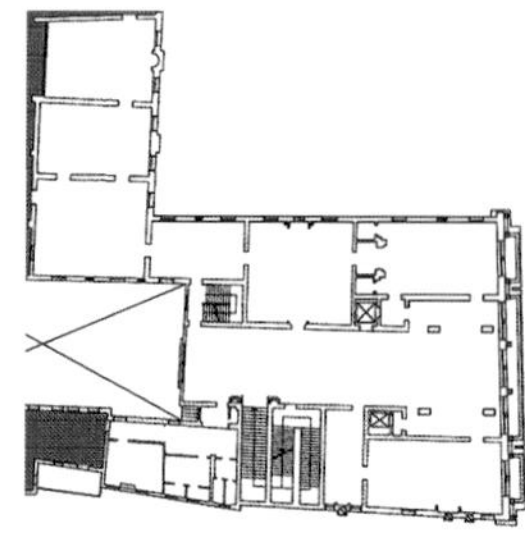

architects
Mauro Codussi

type
residential

construction
1481-1509

32. Housing Project in Cannaregio (Former Saffa Area)

Cannaregio
30100 Venice

external viewing only

1, 2, 2/, N >
Ferrovia A
1, 2, 2/, 5.2, N >
Ferrovia B
4.2, 5.1, 5.2 > Crea

Stazione di Venezia Santa Lucia

The housing project in the former Saffa industrial area in Cannaregio, designed in 1984 by Vittorio Gregotti, represents one of the most important examples of modern residential construction in the historic Venetian urban fabric. Part of an INA-Casa program, the complex is composed of a group of buildings that repropose typical Venetian urban elements like bell towers, narrow alleys, and courtyards, but in Rationalist style. Gregotti decided to use compact volumes and a restrained architectural style, where the residential blocks are positioned along pedestrian routes that create intermediary spaces destined for social contact. The exposed brick facades establish a visual and material link with the local traditional building style despite the clearly modern rational design. Regular symmetrical loggias and window openings provide a dynamic flexible quality, erasing all signs of formal rigidity. The project stands out for its capacity to harmoniously combine inhabitants' needs and urban quality, using architecture as an instrument to rehabilitate a marginal peripheral area without sacrificing its strong project design character. In this sense, the Cannaregio housing project demonstrates how a rationalist approach can be applied in a sensitive way, maintaining its links with history while responding to present-day needs.

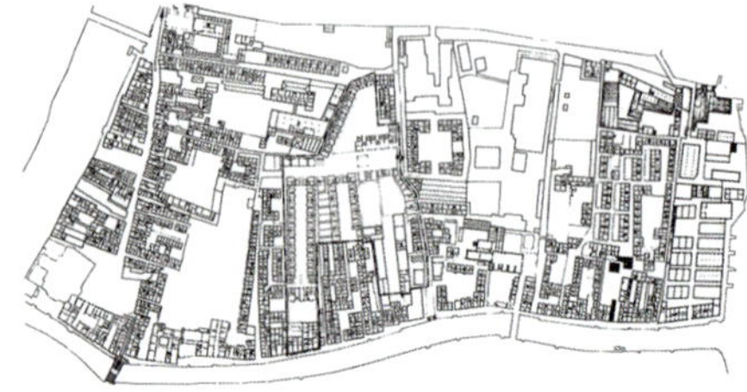

© Petr Šmídek

architects
Vittorio Gregotti

type
residential

construction
1984

33. Ghetto of Venice

Campo del Ghetto Nuovo,
Campo del Magazzen 2882
30121 Venice

external viewing only
+39 041 5246 083
ghettovenezia@operalaboratori.com
www.ghettovenezia.com

4.1, 4.2, 5.1, 5.2, A > Guglie

The Ghetto of Venice, established in 1516, is one of the first enclosed Jewish quarters in history. It became a unique urban model for the forced coexistence of different communities inside a densely built-up urban fabric. The quarter was developed in a limited area in the Cannaregio sestiere and was then divided up into the New Ghetto, Old Ghetto and Newer Ghetto, composed of tall, layered buildings, constructed as a result of having to house a growing population in a limited space. The Ghetto architecture is renowned for its tall buildings, as high as seven floors, unusual for Venice. This increase in dense construction was in response to restrictions imposed by the Venetian administration which limited expansion of the Jewish quarter. The apparently plain facades conceal a rich stratification of various architectures, including five historical synagogues, hidden within the pre-existent architecture to respect the urban building standards of the period. As well as its architectural importance, the Venetian Ghetto represents a site of remarkable historical and social value, witness to centuries of cultural cohabitation, segregation, and integration between the Jewish community and the city of Venice.

© Boris-B / Shutterstock.com

architects
-

type
residential

construction
1516 ca.

34. Former Teatro Italia

Calle de l'Anconeta 1944
30121 Venice

open to the public
+39 041 2440 243

 **1, 2, N** > S. Marcuola Casino

Designed by the architect, Giovanni Sardi, and built in 1916, Teatro Italia represents one of the most refined expressions of Liberty architecture in Venice. Situated in the Cannaregio sestiere, the building is integrated within a dense urban context but stands out for its refined facade and the elegance of its decorative elements. The dialogue between past and present is one of the principal characteristics of Sardi's style, combining Gothic inspiration with the light dynamic design of the Liberty period. The central element of the facade features a large three-foiled window, framed with ornamental motifs that highlight the vertical effect of the building, making it a visual reference point along Strada Nova. The interior of the theatre, originally designed also as a cinema, was decorated with frescoes and wrought iron elements in pure Liberty style. Following a long period of neglect and abandon, the theatre was restored and converted to house a supermarket, while maintaining its original structure and architectural style intact. This intervention has enabled the city to recover an important example of early 20th century architecture, preserving its artistic and historic value.

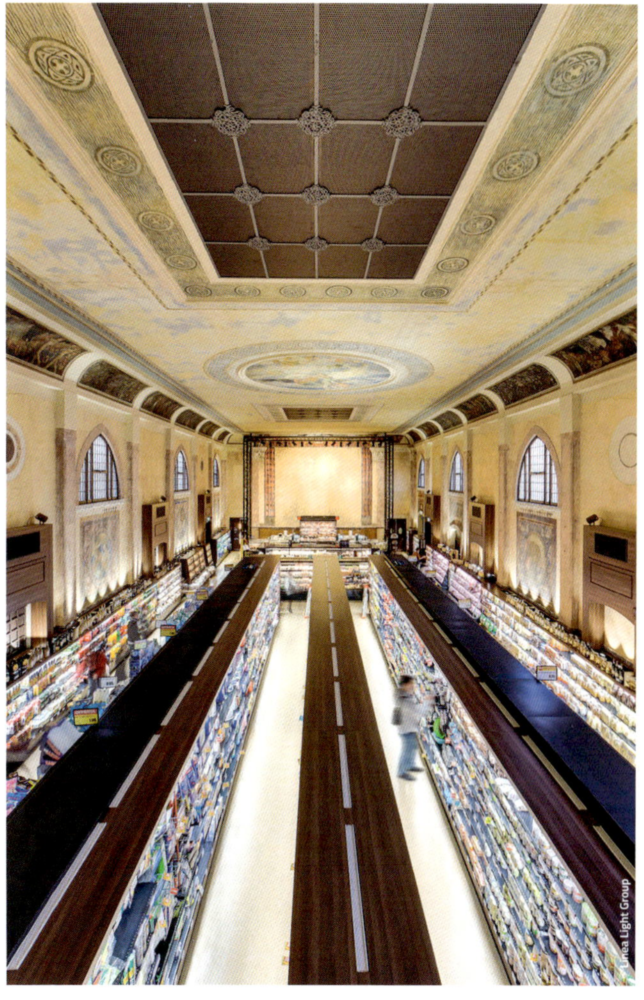

Linea Light Group

architects
Giovanni Sardi

type
commercial

construction
1916

35. Church of Santa Maria dei Miracoli

Campiello dei Miracoli
30121 Venice

Mon - Sat / 10.30 am - 5 pm
+39 041 2750 462
info@chorusvenezia.org
www.chorusvenezia.org/visita/chiesa-di-santa-maria-dei-miracoli

 **1, 2, 2/, N** > Rialto

The church of Santa Maria dei Miracoli (Saint Mary of Miracles), designed by Pietro Lombardo and completed in 1489, is one of the jewels of the Venetian Renaissance. Located in the Cannaregio sestiere, the church is renowned for its compact form and exquisitely decorative beauty, making it unique among the architectural monuments in the city. The exterior is completely clad in polychrome marble with a refined play of geometrical inlay and relief that add to the sculptural quality of the facade. A triumphal arch and semicircular tympanum accentuate the central entrance in the main facade. The use of marble from ancient Roman buildings gives the building a sense of continuity with classical architecture. The interior features a single nave with a barrel-vaulted roof decorated with a gilded coffered ceiling, creating a wonderful glowing effect. The main altar, adorned with a delicate icon of the Virgin, is inserted within a semi-circular apse reminiscent of early Christian architecture. The relationship between space and decoration was created with great attention to produce an almost metaphysical effect. The church is a masterpiece of refined harmony, combining architecture, sculpture and decoration, a magnificent expression of the artistic elegance of the Venetian Renaissance.

© NEKOMURA / Shutterstock.com

architects
Pietro Lombardo

type
religious

construction
1480-1489

36. Campo Santi Giovanni e Paolo

Campo Santi Giovanni e Paolo
30122 Venice

external viewing only

4.1, 4.2, 5.1, 5.2, 22, B
> Ospedale

Campo Santi Giovanni e Paolo, is one of the largest and most spectacular squares in Venice, and represents an exceptional example of Venetian urban space, dominated by the massive Basilica dei Santi Giovanni e Paolo and the equestrian momument in honour of Bartolomeo Colleoni di Verrocchio. The construction of the basilica began in the 13th century and was completed in the 15th century, and is one of the maximum examples of Venetian Gothic style. The brick facade features a deep portal entrance topped by a large pointed arch, leading to the majestic interior with its high cross vaulted ceiling, and rich collection of memorial monuments to the Doges of Venice. In front of the church, an equestrian monument to Colleoni created in 1483, is one of the masterpieces of Renaissance sculpture, with a dynamic composition that exalts the figure of the ruler. Overlooking the square is the former Scuola Grande di San Marco, which houses a public hospital today; its wonderful Renaissance facade is decorated with marble relief work and Palladian windows. Campo Santi Giovanni e Paolo is a space with a strong symbolic and historical value, where religious, public, and military architecture coexist to create one of the most spectacular backdrops in the city.

architects
-

type
public space

construction
13th–15th c.

37. Fondazione Querini Stampalia – Expansion

Campo Santa Maria Formosa 5252
30122 Venice

Tue - Sun / 10 am - 6 pm
+39 041 2711 411
fondazione@querinistampalia.org
www.querinistampalia.org

1, 5.2, N > S. Marco-San Zaccaria "E"-"F"

The Fondazione Querini Stampalia intervention by Carlo Scarpa (1959-63) is one of the most emblematic architectural projects of the 20th century, where a profound respect for the historical context is interwoven with innovative design. Located in a 16th century palace in the heart of Venice, this project is remarkable for its attention to detail and its sensitive use of materials. Scarpa redesigned the internal spaces and access to water using an approach that enhances the continuity between the architecture and the urban landscape. The internal canal system on the ground floor, designed to resolve problems of high water levels, and the internal courtyard, with its elegant stone, bronze and mosaic composition, represents a combination of tradition and modernity. The interior layout is designed to create a constant flow of light and movement, thanks to refined spatial solutions and choice of materials, such as marble, wood and glass. The garden was conceived as a microcosm, harmoniously integrating natural and artificial elements. Between 1982 and 1997, Valeriano Pastor applied original architectural solutions for his interventions: he designed a curved wooden staircase and nautically inspired porthole windows, a walkway between the library and book depository, and a large wood and metal door in dialogue with the gate by Carlo Scarpa.

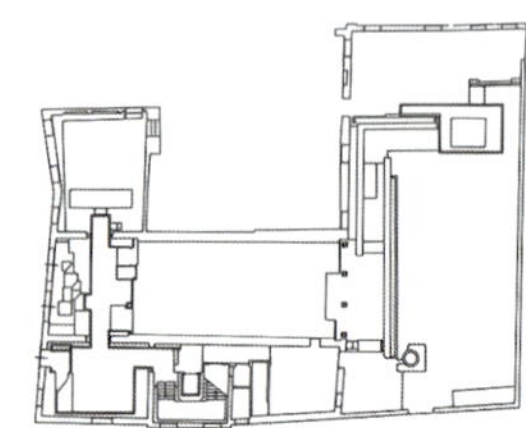

Courtesy Fondazione Querini Stampalia

© Linea Light Group

architects
Carlo Scarpa

type
cultural

construction
1959-1963

Campo Santa Maria Formosa 5252
30122 Venice

Tue - Sun / 10 am - 6 pm
+39 041 2711 411
fondazione@querinistampalia.org
www.querinistampalia.org

1, 5.2, N > S. Marco-San Zaccaria "E"-"F"

Between 1994 and 2013, Mario Botta expanded the building with a project that reflects the historic Venetian style, completing the architecture of the complex without modifying its identity. The intervention involved the creation of new spaces, a bookshop and a café, plus the renewal and reorganisation of the internal layout. The new courtyard features a strict facade, punctuated by regular rows of window openings in traditional Venetian design, but created in contemporary style. Special care was taken to integrate the design with the restoration by Carlo Scarpa. Botta repeated certain elements designed by Scarpa to create an interaction between different periods and architectural styles. Another important intervention is the exhibition space created on the third floor in 2018 by Michele De Lucchi. By eliminating several partitions, the architect was able to recreate a "telescopic" optical effect through a sequence of aligned doorways. As a whole, the Fondazione Querini Stampalia emerges as a masterpiece of equilibrium between historic memory and contemporary design, renewing a sense of space without eradicating its roots.

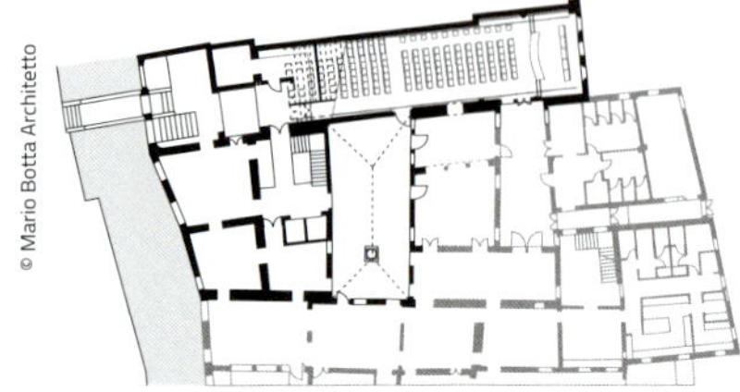

architects
Mario Botta (expansion)

type
cultural

construction
1994-2013

38. Church of San Zaccaria

Campo S. Zaccaria 4693
30122 Venice

Mon - Sat / 10 am - 12.00 am
Sun / 4 pm - 6 pm
+39 041 5221 257

1, 5.2, N > S. Marco-
San Zaccaria "E"-"F"

The church of San Zaccaria is among the oldest in Venice, and one of the masterpieces of the transition between the Gothic and Renaissance periods. It was designed by Mauro Codussi in the latter 15th century. The church was built on the remains of a Medieval basilica, maintaining the layout of the original structure, but with a reinterpretation based on the new principles of classic architecture. The facade is typical of Codussi's design, with its division of superimposed orders and its perfect balance between Gothic and Renaissance styles. The use of white marble and position of the arches create a weightless effect, while the semicircular crowning element was an innovative solution for the period. The triple nave interior features a large presbytery and wonderful painted decorations, including the famous altarpiece of San Zaccaria by Giovanni Bellini (1505), considered one of the greatest examples of Venetian Renaissance painting. The church also houses a crypt, part of the ancient Medieval building, a burial place for many of the Doges. This space, which is often submerged during high water levels, is a fascinating testimony to the historic evolution of the building. San Zaccaria is one of the most refined examples of Venetian transition architecture; a perfect balance between formal innovation and the continuity of traditional design.

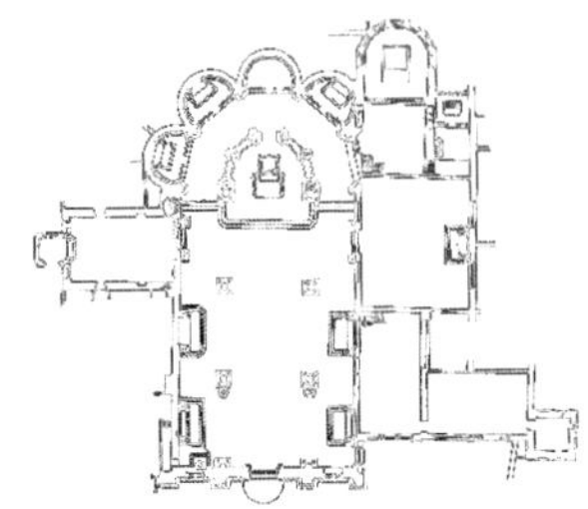

architects
Mauro Codussi

type
religious

construction
1445-1515

39. Bridge of Sighs

Ponte dei Sospiri
30124 Venice

open to the public

www.palazzoducaledivenezia.it

1, 5.2, N > S. Marco-San Zaccaria "E"-"F"
B > S. Marco

The Bridge of Sighs, designed by Antonio Contin and built in 1602, is one of the most iconic bridges in Venice. Built of Istria stone, the bridge connects the Ducal Palace with the Prigioni Nuove (New Prisons), forming the passageway for condemned prisoners as they were led from the Law Courts to the prison cells. The bridge design is in late Renaissance style, with an enclosed structure and grated windows, concealing two narrow internal corridors. Its arched form and bas-relief decoration create a light elegant effect in contrast with its original function. The name, "Bridge of Sighs" comes from the romantic legend according to which prisoners sighed as they saw the lagoon through the grated windows for the last time. This bridge, a symbol of Venice and its history, is an architectural work that summarizes the elegance of Venetian architecture and the dramatic history of its judicial past.

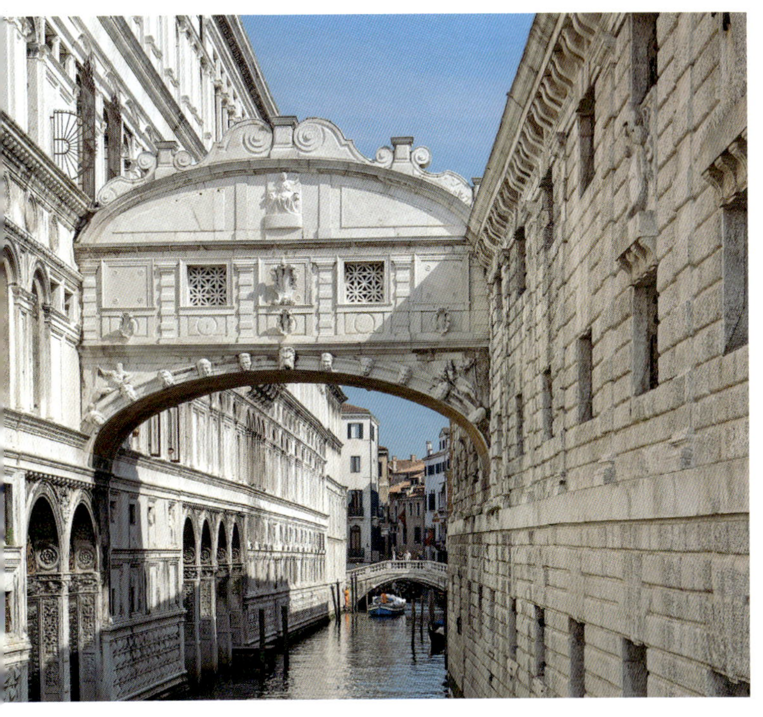

architects
Antonio Contin

type
cultural

construction
1602

40. Ducal Palace

Piazza San Marco 1
30124 Venice

open to the public

www.palazzoducaledivenezia.it

1, 5.2, N > S. Marco-San Zaccaria "E"-"F"
B > S. Marco

The Ducal Palace is the most important public building in Venice, symbol of the power of the Serenissima (Venetian Republic) and masterpiece of Venetian Gothic architecture. The construction began in the 9th century, but the current building mainly dates back to the 14th and 15th centuries, with some interventions in Renaissance and Mannerism style. The building is famous for is amazing visual elegance, obtained through the inversion of its structural configuration: the lower part is composed of loggias with trefoil arches set on columns, while the more solid upper section is lightened by the geometrically patterned cladding in Istrian and Veronese marble. This gives the palace an almost floating effect, intensifying the fusion between architecture and the lagoon. The interior of the palace maintains its monumental atmosphere, like the Great Council Chamber, one of the largest in Europe, decorated with works by Tintoretto, Veronese and Tiziano. The internal courtyard shows a layering of Gothic and Renaissance elements, while the Bridge of Sighs, built in the 17th century, connects the palace to the "New Prison", underlining the dualism between power and justice. The Ducal Palace is a building that embodies the essence of Venice, combining decorative elegance and political function: a perfect synthesis of art and government.

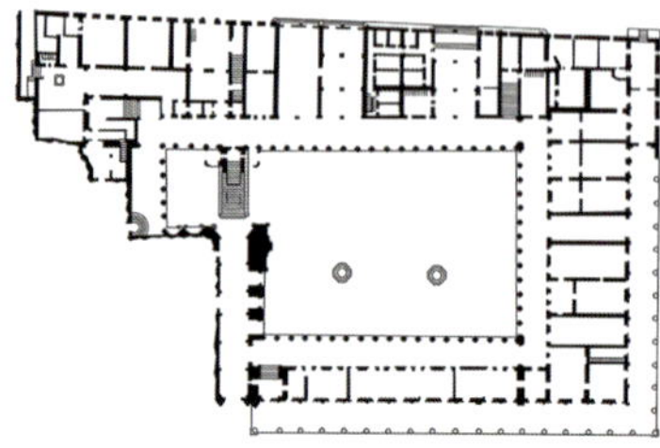

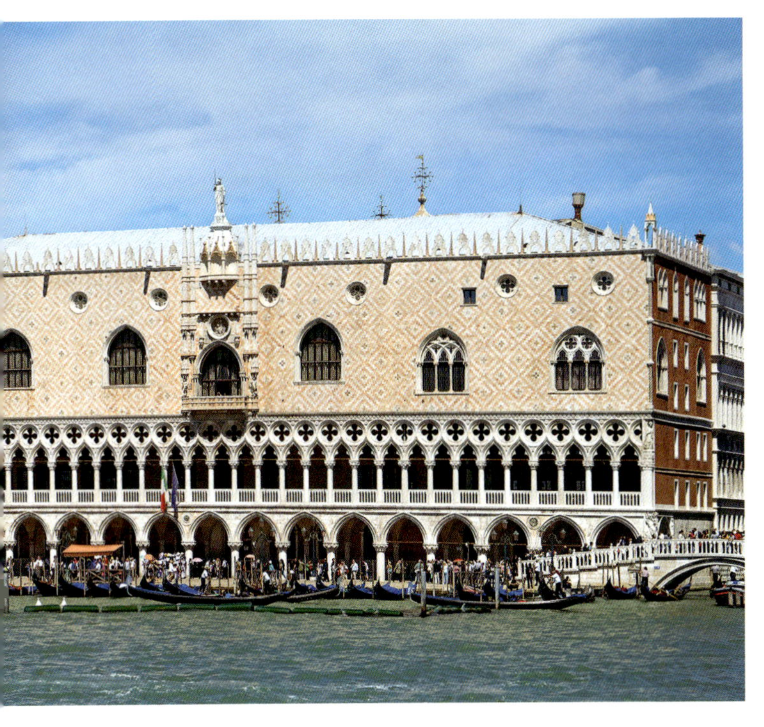

architects	**type**	**construction**
-	cultural	14th-15th c.

41. Saint Mark's Square

Piazza San Marco 328
30124 Venice

open to the public

www.basilicasanmarco.it

1, 5.2, N > S. Marco-San Zaccaria "E"-"F"
B > S. Marco

Saint Mark's Square, the symbolic heart of Venice, and one of the world's most famous urban spaces, is the result of centuries of architectural evolution. The square assumed its current form between the 12th and 18th centuries, and is surrounded by monumental buildings of extraordinary architectural quality: Saint Mark's Basilica, the Bell Tower, the Procuratie Vecchie, the Procuratie Nuove and Napoleonic Wing. Saint Mark's Basilica, built in the 9th century and reconstructed in the 11th century, is the greatest example of Byzantine design in the West. Its five-domed, Greek Cross structure, inspired by the Church of the Holy Apostles in Constantinople, is enriched with amazing mosaic decorations narrating the sacred history and the power of the Serenissima Republic. The facade features arches and loggias; a palimpsest of Eastern and Gothic influences, enriched with sculptures and multicoloured marble inserts. The composition of the square is a perfect balance between urban space and monumental architecture, a place where Venetian history is manifested in its most iconic form.

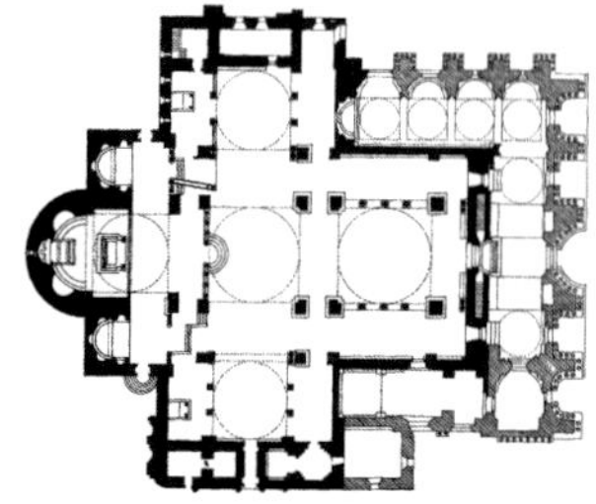

© Stockbym/ Shutterstock.com

architects
-

type
public space

construction
9th c.

42. Procuratie Vecchie – Restoration

Piazza San Marco 105
30124 Venice

summer timetable
Mon, Wed - Sun /
10 am - 7 pm
winter timetablev
Mon, Wed - Sun /
10 am - 6 pm

 **B** > S. Marco

Following years of research and meticulous intervention, David Chipperfield Architects Milan's restoration of the Procuratie Vecchie was completed in 2022. This historic complex, located along the northern side of Saint Mark's Square, is one of the most important architectural symbols of Venice and, thanks to Chipperfield's intervention, it has been returned to the city in a revived version, but one which is deeply respectful of its historic value. The project focussed on renovating the interiors, converted to house office spaces for the Fondazione Generali and The Human Safety Net, exhibition spaces and areas open to the public. The restoration involved the application of ancient, traditional, local construction techniques. Venetian craftsmen created marble pastellone and terrazzo floorings, and marmorino, whitewash, terra cotta and cocciopesto finishes for the walls and ceilings. Traditional materials were used, combined with contemporary details, like the metal window frames and integrated lighting systems. One of the main aspects of the project was to upgrade the vertical and horizontal connections in the building to improve accessibility and functionality. The project leaves space to reveal the monumental elements of the original structure, using contemporary interventions that give the historic building new life and function, in a projection towards the future without betraying its cultural and symbolic importance.

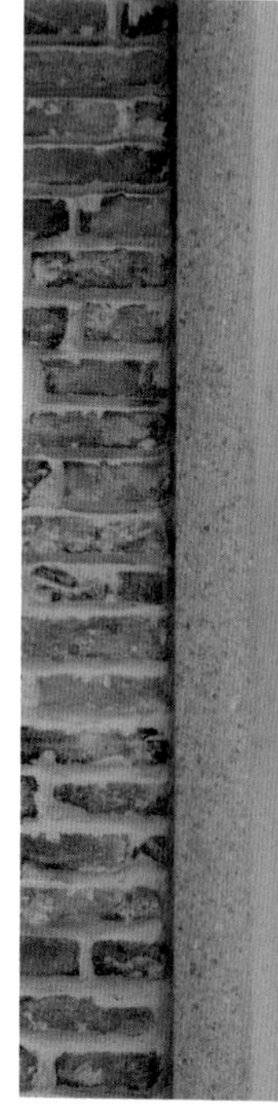

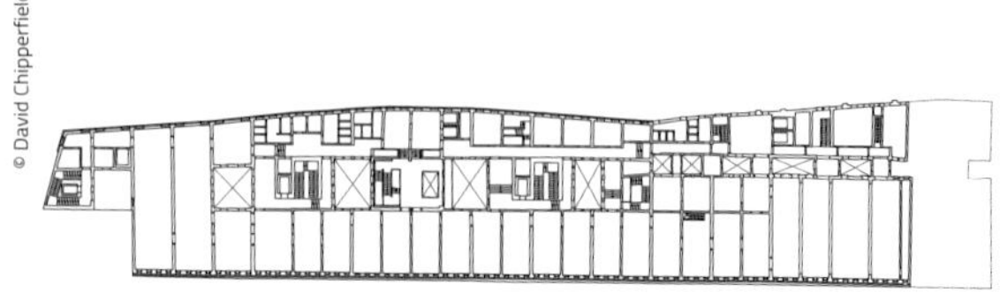

© Alessandra Chemollo. Courtesy David Chipperfield Architects

architects
David Chipperfield Architects
Milan

type
multi-purpose

construction
2022

43. Negozio Olivetti

Piazza San Marco 101
30124 Venice

Tue - Sun / 10 am - 6.30 pm
+39 041 5228 387
fainegoziolivetti@
fondoambiente.it
www.fondoambiente.it/luoghi/
negozio-olivetti

B > S. Marco Giardinetti
A, B > San Marco
Vallaresso ACTV

The Negozio Olivetti, created by Carlo Scarpa and finished in 1958, is a masterpiece of modern design in the heart of Saint Mark's Square in Venice. This intervention, commissioned by Adriano Olivetti, is a remarkable project for its transformation of a small retail space into an architectural work of art celebrating the union of tradition and innovation. Scarpa used choice, premium materials – marble, bronze, wood and glass – to create a refined but functional environment, designed to showcase Olivetti products and to offer the viewer a unique aesthetic experience. The iconic element of the project is the suspended staircase in the entrance, composed of marble and bronze steps that seem to float in space, visually connecting the ground level with the upper floor. The interior is designed with meticulous attention to detail: the Venetian terrazzo walls and flooring are decorated with geometrical inserts reflecting the strict elegance of Olivetti design. Glass panels and reflecting surfaces create a play of light and transparency, giving a sense of depth in the contained space. The Negozio Olivetti is not simply a commercial space, but a manifesto of Scarpa's design aesthetic: architecture able to transform every single element into a work of integrated design where formal beauty is combined with functional purpose, and respect for the historical context of Venice.

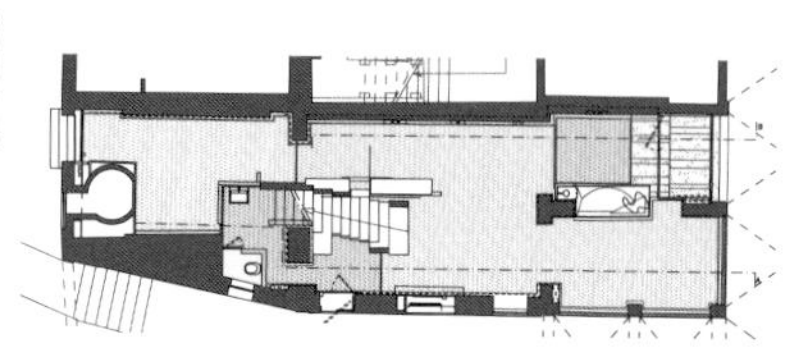

architects
Carlo Scarpa

type
cultural

construction
1958

44. Biblioteca Nazionale Marciana

Piazza San Marco 7
30124 Venice

winter timetable
Mon - Sun / 10 am - 5 pm
summer timetable
Mon - Sun / 10 am - 6 pm
+39 041 2407 211
b-marc@cultura.gov.it
www.
bibliotecanazionalemarciana.
cultura.gov.it

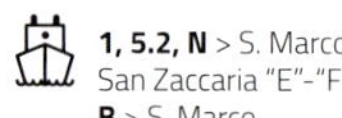
1, 5.2, N > S. Marco-San Zaccaria "E"-"F"
B > S. Marco

The Biblioteca Nazionale Marciana, designed by Jacopo Sansovino and completed by Vincenzo Scamozzi, is one of the most quintessential works of the Venetian Classical Renaissance period. Situated along the side of Saint Mark's Square opposite the Doge's Palace, The Marciana was conceived as a celebration of humanistic teachings and a tribute to the cultural power of the Serenissima. The building is composed of two orders: the first features a long portico of Ionic pillars topped with rounded arches, while the second forms a loggia with Corinthian pillars and richly carved decorations. The building displays an elegant harmony with its regular sequence of openings and the use of polychrome marble; it is crowned with an elaborate top floor decorated with statues to increase the monumental effect. The interior forms a sumptuous space with frescoes and decorations to enhance the library's role as a temple of knowledge. The intervention by Scamozzi, who completed the structure after the death of Sansovino, remained faithful to the original project, emphasising its symmetry and proportions. The Biblioteca Marciana is a masterful example of Renaissance architecture, perfectly integrated within the monumental fabric of Saint Mark's Square, bearing witness to the 16th century Venetian passion for culture.

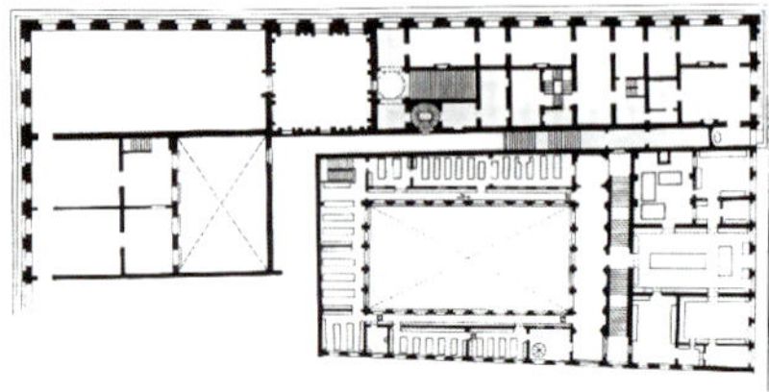

architects
Jacopo Sansovino,
Vincenzo Scamozzi

type
cultural

construction
1537-1588

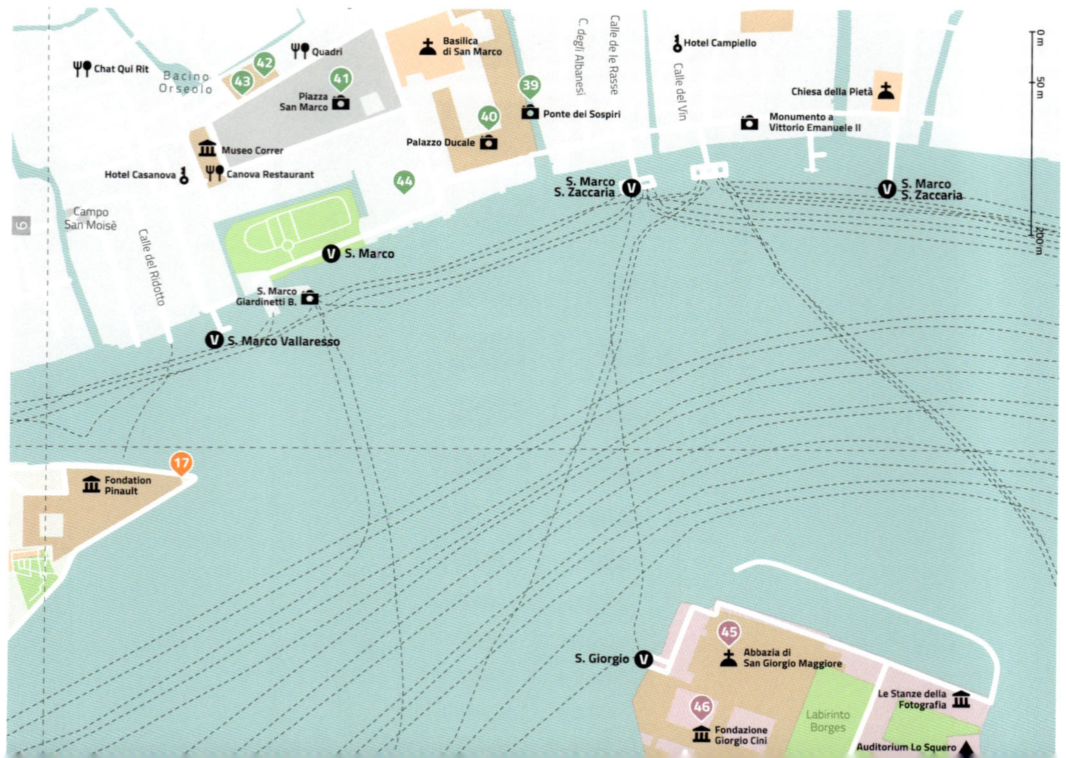
0 m
50 m
200 m
Chat Qui Rit
Bacino Orseolo
43
42
Quadri
41
Piazza San Marco
Basilica di San Marco
39
Ponte dei Sospiri
40
Palazzo Ducale
C. degli Albanesi
Calle de le Rasse
Calle del Vin
Hotel Campiello
Chiesa della Pietà
Monumento a Vittorio Emanuele II
Museo Correr
Hotel Casanova
Canova Restaurant
44
S. Marco S. Zaccaria
S. Marco S. Zaccaria
9
Campo San Moisè
Calle del Ridotto
S. Marco
S. Marco Giardinetti B.
S. Marco Vallaresso
17
Fondation Pinault
S. Giorgio
45
Abbazia di San Giorgio Maggiore
46
Fondazione Giorgio Cini
Labirinto Borges
Le Stanze della Fotografia
Auditorium Lo Squero

Giudecca – Lido – Sacca Sesola

45. Basilica of San Giorgio Maggiore
46. Fondazione Giorgio Cini
47. Vatican Chapels (Island of San Giorgio Maggiore)
48. Teatro Verde
49. Le Zitelle or Spinsters' Church
50. Apartment Buildings in Campo di Marte – ATER / Condominio Aymonino Housing Project
51. Campo di Marte / Condominio Álvaro Siza Housing Project

0 m
50 m
200 m
Hilton
55
Hilton Molino Stucky Venice
Fondamenta S. Biagio
C. Larga dei Lavraneri
Spazio Punch
54
Giudecca Palanca
56
Rio di San Biagio
Fondamenta de le Convertite
10
Calle del Pistor
C. S. Cosimo
Calle CLunga dell'Accademia dei Nobili
Calle Nicoli
Calle dell'Olio
Palazzo Veneziano
53
Calle Cantiere
Calle Scuola
Teatro Junghans
Rio delle Convertite
F

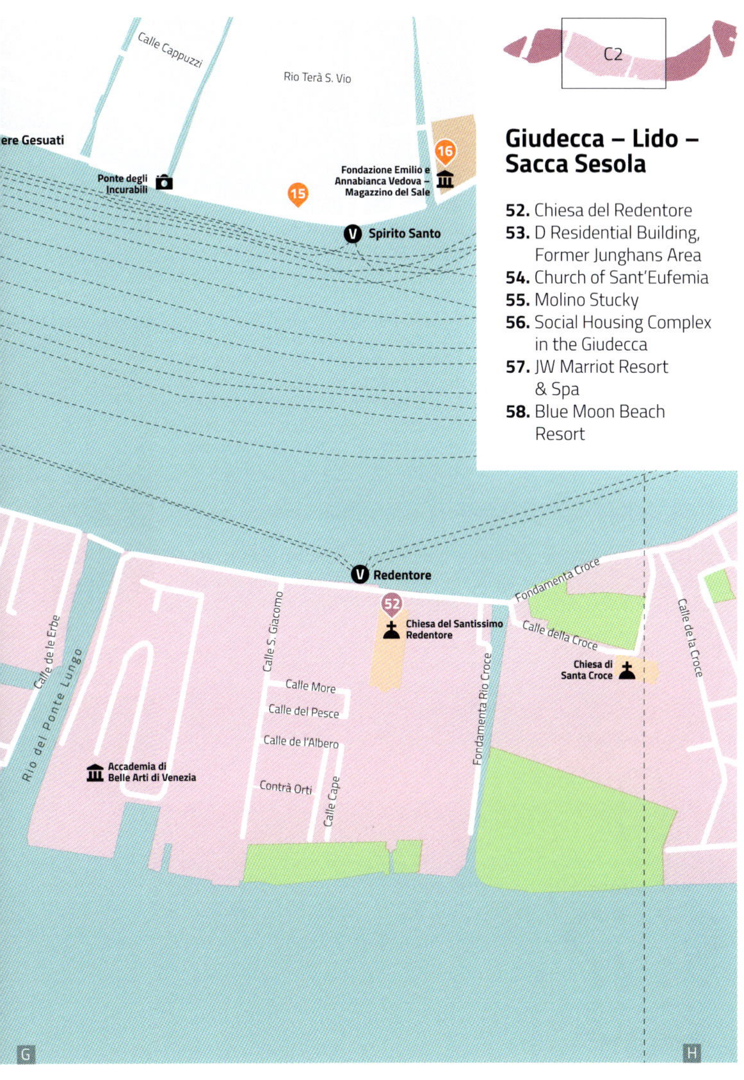

Giudecca – Lido – Sacca Sesola

52. Chiesa del Redentore
53. D Residential Building, Former Junghans Area
54. Church of Sant'Eufemia
55. Molino Stucky
56. Social Housing Complex in the Giudecca
57. JW Marriot Resort & Spa
58. Blue Moon Beach Resort

45. Basilica of San Giorgio Maggiore

Isola di San Giorgio Maggiore 2
30124 Venice

Mon - Sun / 9 am - 6 pm
+39 375 6323 595
visite@abbaziasangiorgio.it
www.abbaziasangiorgio.it

 **2, N** > S. Giorgio

The Basilica of San Giorgio Maggiore, designed by Andrea Palladio and completed after his death by Vincenzo Scamozzi in 1610, is one of the Renaissance masterpieces of Venice. Located on the island bearing its name, opposite Saint Mark's Square, the church is famous for its majestic facade in white Istria marble, an example of the perfect synthesis of Classical and Monumental architecture. Palladio designed the building according to the principles of proportion and harmony, based on the models of ancient Rome, translated in Christian style. The facade features a double order of columns and pilasters, with a central tympanum to accentuate the entrance and create a dynamic perspective effect. The interior, with a triple nave, Latin cross layout, is dominated by natural light filtered through the large openings in the dome drum and clerestory galleries, emphasising the space and architectural purity. The main altar is enriched with the famous *Last Supper* painting by Tintoretto, in perfect harmony with the austerity and solemn atmosphere of the environment. The basilica is a model of perfect integration of architecture, light, and religious symbolism, exemplifying the Palladian concept of beauty and rational design applied to religious architecture.

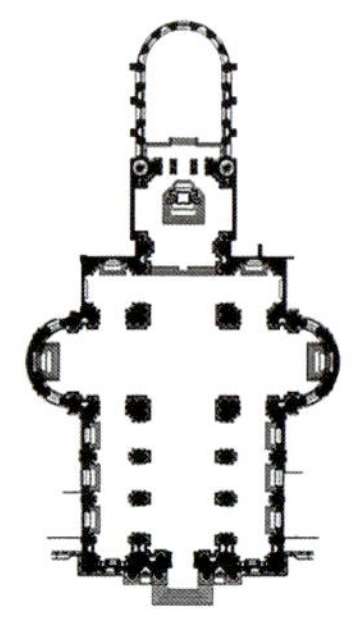

architects
Andrea Palladio,
Vincenzo Scamozzi

type
religious

construction
1560-1610

46. Fondazione Giorgio Cini

San Giorgio Maggiore
30133 Venice

open to the public
+39 041 2710 211
info@www.cini.it
www.cini.it

 **2, N** > S. Giorgio

The Fondazione Giorgio Cini, established on the island of San Giorgio Maggiore in 1951, is a superb example of architectural restoration and functional adaptation. Originally a 10th century Benedictine Monastery, the complex was severely damaged during the Napoleonic occupation and the Second World War. The project by Angelo Scattolin and Luigi Vietti was aimed at restoring the cultural and spiritual focus, transforming it into a centre for research and advanced education. The restoration project maintained the monastic structure, enhancing the cloister and internal spaces with an approach that creates a balance between tradition and innovation. The buildings now house libraries, conference rooms, and exhibition spaces. The lighting and materials were researched with great care to preserve the historical character of the building while focusing on upgrading the foundation's new functions. Strict attention was paid to the relationship with the lagoon landscape, with the skilful use of glimpses and openings to accentuate the bond between the architecture and the water. Today, the foundation represents a model for cultural restoration, where historic architecture becomes a driving force for new intellectual vitality.

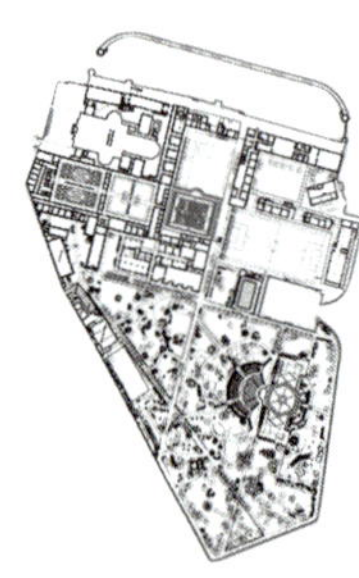

© Irene Bigolin

architects
Angelo Scattolin, Luigi Vietti

type
cultural

construction
1951

47. Vatican Chapels (Island of San Giorgio Maggiore)

San Giorgio Maggiore
30133 Venice

open to the public
+39 366 4202 181
info@visitcini.com
www.cini.it

2, N > S. Giorgio

The Vatican Chapels, designed for the 16th International Architecture Biennale of Venice (2018), form a unique project, where contemporary architecture coexists with the concept of the Sacred. Conceived as a reinterpretation of the chapel in the woods by Gunnar Asplund, these temporary structures were integrated within the landscape of the Island of San Giorgio Maggiore, offering an immersive itinerary in a spiritual environment in the midst of nature. The project was entrusted to ten international architects, and the chapels were designed to explore the concept of meditation and reflection in various ways, through innovative forms, materials and spatial solutions. The most iconic project was designed by Norman Foster (following page), who created a suspended steel and wooden structure, featuring intersecting wooden beams to filter light and emphasise a sense of weightlessness and spirituality. Francesco Cellini proposed a geometrically pure white concrete structure, a plain simple design where natural light plays a central role, creating a strong contrast between solids and voids. Smiljan Radic created a monolithic chapel in blocks of raw stone, recalling Romanesque architecture with an archaic atmosphere, while Eduardo Souto de Moura was inspired by the idea of ruins, assembling stone elements that seem to belong to an unknown time, in communication with memory and nature. The concept of a refuge was the main element for the project

© Laurian Ghinitoiu

architects
Flores i Prats Arquitectes, Foster + Partners, Teronobu Fujimori, Andrew Berman Architect, Sean Godsell Architects, Francesco Cellini, Carla Juaçaba, Eduardo Souto de Moura, Magnani Pelzel Architetti Associati, Smiljan Radic, Javier Corvalán

type
cultural

construction
2018

San Giorgio Maggiore
30133 Venice

open to the public
+39 366 4202 181
info@visitcini.com
www.cini.it

2, N > S. Giorgio

by Sean Godsell, who created a chapel using perforated metal panels, to form a permeable shell between interior and exterior, suggesting a sense of protection. Carla Juaçaba took the concept of structural simplicity to the extreme with a design reduced to four metal crossed beams, eliminating any walls to create direct interaction between the sacred space and the surrounding landscape. Javier Corvalán (following page) proposed an experimental approach with an inverted cylindrical chapel that reverses the perception of space and directs the view towards the altar through sloping curved surfaces. This group of Vatican Chapels offers the visitor an unusual architectural and meditative experience, where formal research is combined with spiritual reflection, creating a "pilgrimage" that inspires contemplation. This project demonstrates how contemporary architecture can reinterpret the sense of spirituality with innovative design, while maintaining a profound connection with tradition and nature.

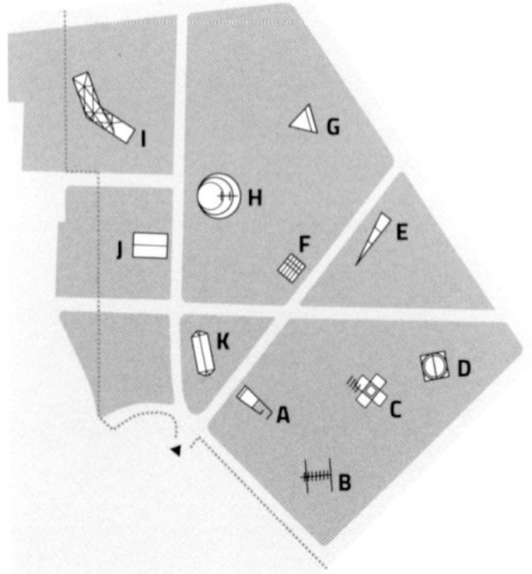

A. Eduardo Souto de Moura
B. Carla Juaçaba
C. Sean Godsell Architects
D. Smiljan Radic
E. Flores i Prats Arquitectes
F. Francesco Cellini
G. Andrew Berman Architect
H. Javier Corvalán
I. Foster + Partners
J. Teronobu Fujimori
K. Magnani Pelzel Architetti Associati

© Isabella Peruzzi

architects
Flores i Prats Arquitectes, Foster + Partners, Teronobu Fujimori, Andrew Berman Architect, Sean Godsell Architects, Francesco Cellini, Carla Juaçaba, Eduardo Souto de Moura, Magnani Pelzel Architetti Associati, Smiljan Radic, Javier Corvalán

type
cultural

construction
2018

48. Teatro Verde

San Giorgio Maggiore
30100 Venice

open to the public
+39 366 4202 181
info@visitcini.com
www.cini.it

 **2, N** > S. Giorgio

The Teatro Verde, designed by Luigi Vietti and Angelo Scattolin in 1954, is a structure unique in the Venetian panorama: an open-air theatre on the Island of San Giorgio Maggiore, set in a landscape of exceptional beauty. This spectacular space, in the form of a classical amphitheatre, unites nature and architecture, blending harmoniously to enhance the genius loci of the island. The theatre structure is based on a semicircular layout, with terraced stone seating that slopes gently towards the stage. The project took advantage of the natural topography of the site, integrating the surrounding vegetation as part of the theatrical backdrop. The construction materials, including brick and local stone, give the theatre a restrained but elegant atmosphere. The location of the Teatro Verde, with the Bacino di San Marco in the background, offers a natural panorama that enhances each theatrical performance, creating a lasting experience between the performing arts and the landscape. This project is a wonderful example of how architecture can enhance a natural environment, by proposing a cultural space that blends with its surroundings, delicately and with respect.

architects
Angelo Scattolin, Luigi Vietti

type
cultural

construction
1954

49. Le Zitelle or Spinsters' Church

Fondamenta Zitelle 33
30133 Venice

external viewing only

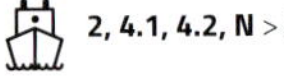

2, 4.1, 4.2, N > Zitelle

The church of Santa Maria della Presentazione, known as "The Spinsters" (zitelle), was one of Andrea Palladio's later works, designed around 1576 and completed after his death. Located on the Giudecca island, the church is part of a complex established to take in young women without dowries (hence the name "spinsters"). The Palladian architectural style is obvious in the purity of its proportions and spatial clarity, in an original interpretation of traditional Venetian churches. The Istria stone facade features a tympanum bourne by four Corinthian half pilasters that emphasise the vertical and monumental effect. The interior is a single large central space with a barrel vaulted roof, while the dome, set on a high drum structure, captures natural light, accentuating the open space and solemnity of the setting. Two side chapels flank the main altar, providing the space with a deeper perspective. The church is famous for its clean, pure style and well-balanced layout, where the geometrical clarity instils a sense of spirituality. The "Spinsters' Church" is a perfect synthesis of a philanthropic function and architectural beauty, a confirmation of Palladio's prodigy in his reinterpretation of the traditional Venetian style.

architects
Andrea Palladio

type
religious

construction
1574-1588

50. Apartment Buildings in Campo di Marte – ATER / Condominio Aymonino Housing Project

Giudecca 972
30133 Venice

external viewing only

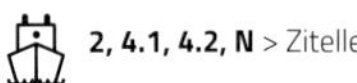

The ATER social housing complex in Campo di Marte, designed in the 1980s by Carlo Aymonino and Aldo Rossi, is part of an urban redevelopment plan, determined by the transformation of the former Junghans industrial area. The project stands out for its design approach that combines rational style while paying close attention to the symbolic value of the historic city. The layout of the complex is based on an orthogonal plan, in which the buildings are arranged around open spaces that recall the structure of the characteristic Venetian campiello. Aymonino and Rossi reinterpreted these traditional local elements, transforming them into communal spaces to promote and encourage social contact and a sense of belonging. The facades reflect a simple but monumental style, featuring alternating solids and voids in classical proportions. The use of brick and exposed concrete provides an austere but solid appearance in harmony with the local Venetian environment. The interiors cater to all the needs of contemporary living, with careful attention to the organisation of space and quality of natural light. This project is impressive for its capacity to combine formal experimentation with profound sensitivity to social aspects, proposing a residential model that focusses on the collective social identity without sacrificing architectural quality.

© Petr Šmídek

architects
Carlo Aymonino, Aldo Rossi

type
residential

construction
1980-1986

51. Campo di Marte / Condominio Álvaro Siza Housing Project

Calle de l'Asilo Mason 962
30133 Venice

external viewing only

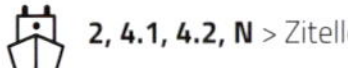
2, 4.1, 4.2, N > Zitelle

The public housing project in Campo di Marte, designed by Álvaro Siza in 1998, represents a skilful combination of Rationalist architecture and careful attention to the specific characteristics of the Venetian context. Located near the ponte della Libertà, the housing complex is part of an urban renewal plan that transformed the former industrial area into a new residential quarter. Siza arranged the buildings following a strict layout that reflects the surrounding urban fabric, but without sacrificing its personal formal autonomy. The buildings are arranged to form a central courtyard, providing a communal space in a contemporary version of the traditional Venetian campiello. The plain geometrical facades feature regular rows of window openings, creating harmonious visual rhythm. Local traditional construction is reflected in the materials like the light coloured plaster and tiled roofing, but expressed in a design style that excludes any form of imitation. Very careful attention was paid to functional design for the interiors, with well-planned layouts that focussed on natural light and generous space. Siza's intervention in Campo di Marte is not limited to a residential building project, but is a contribution to reflection on contemporary lifestyle quality where the architectural project acts as a mediator between historical memory and construction innovation.

© Petr Šmídek

architects
Álvaro Siza

type
residential

construction
1998

52. Chiesa del Redentore

Giudecca 194
30133 Venice

Mon - Sat / 10.30 am - 5 pm
+39 041 2750 462
info@chorusvenezia.org
chorusvenezia.org

2, 4.1, 4.2, N >
Redentore

The Chiesa del Redentore, by Andrea Palladio, built between 1577 and 1592, is one of the most powerful expressions of Renaissance classicism in Venice. Commissioned by the Senate of the Venetian Republic in thanksgiving for deliverance from the plague of 1575-77, the church rises in solemn splendour on the island of the Giudecca, providing the city with an unavoidable visual and symbolic reminder. The facade, inspired by the temples of ancient Rome, features Corinthian columns capped with a large pediment to mark the entrance. The single nave church with barrel vaulted ceilings, has three chapels on either side and is crowned with a monumental central dome to convey a sense of rising spirituality. Natural light filters through the openings in the drum and the counter-facade accentuating the pure white internal surfaces and strictly geometrical design. Palladio designed the Redentore as a work of architectural and theological perfection where symmetry and proportions were used to express its sacred nature. Today, the church is still the heart of the traditional Festa del Redentore, an event that bears witness to the deep bonds between architecture, collective memory and local identity.

architects
Andrea Palladio

type
religious

construction
1577-1592

53. D Residential Building, Former Junghans Area

Giudecca
30133 Venice

external viewing only

2, 4.1, N >
Giudecca Palanca A
2, 4.2, N >
Giudecca Palanca B

The residential quarter built on the former Junghans site was designed by Cino Zucchi and completed in 2003. It is one of the most important urban renewal ventures in the Venice-Mestre region. Built in the area of a famous former manufacturing plant, the project has transformed an abandoned industrial site into a residential and cultural complex, creating a new balance between public and private spaces. The architectural solutions are striking for the variety of building sizes and the materials adopted. The buildings are arranged around courtyards and planted areas, and feature modular facades with brick cladding and metal panels that create a play of solids and voids, light and shade. These details are not simply decorative, but are designed in accordance with environmental sustainability criteria, and to improve energy efficiency. The walkways and internal piazzas in the public spaces were designed to encourage social contact and integration among the residents, transforming the quarter into a lively, welcoming neighbourhood. Zucchi's project, of which Building D is representative, represents a contemporary design model able to reinterpret the historical urban fabric with sensitivity and innovative ideas.

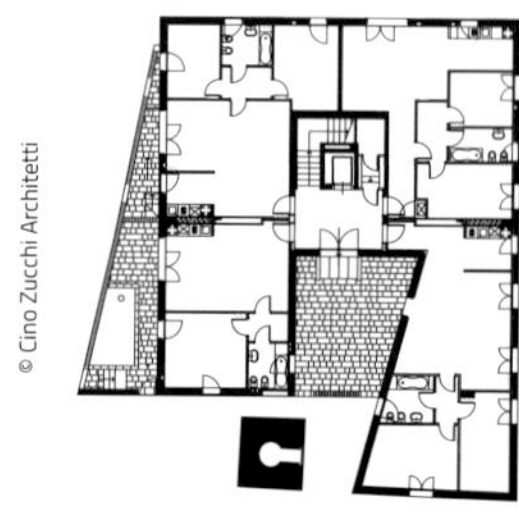

© Pietro Savorelli. Courtesy Cino Zucchi Architetti

architects	**type**	**construction**
Cino Zucchi Architetti	residential	2003

54. Church of Sant'Eufemia

Fondamenta Sant'Eufemia 679
30133 Venice

open to the public

2, 4.1, N > Giudecca Palanca A
2, 4.2, N > Giudecca Palanca B

Dating back to the 11th century, the church of Sant'Eufemia on the Giudecca island, is one of the oldest examples of Venetian religious architecture. The building has undergone numerous interventions over the centuries, but the structure has maintained a blend of Romanesque, Gothic and Renaissance styles, bearing witness to the historic and artistic evolution of the city. The plain, strict facade features a large portal surmounted by a rose window, typical of Gothic architecture. Marble pillars divide the interior into three naves, with a wooden truss ceiling that reflects the style of Early Christian basilicas. The polygonal apse is decorated with frescos, and the exquisite side chapels bear witness to the Renaissance influence during later interventions. The church occupies an unobtrusive position close to the water, creating an atmosphere of spirituality and meditation. Despite the modifications and restorations over time, Sant'Eufemia has maintained its unique architectural identity, expressing the stratified and complex character of Venetian history.

architects
-

type
religious

construction
11th-18th c.

55. Molino Stucky

Giudecca 810
30133 Venice

external viewing only

2, 4.2, N >
Sacca Fisola B
2, 4.2, N > Giudecca
Palanca B

Molino Stucky, the imposing industrial complex located on the island of Giudecca, is one of the most important examples of Neo-Gothic architecture used in manufacturing buildings in Venice. Designed by the German architect, Ernst Wullekopf, at the end of the 19th century as a flour mill and pasta manufacturing plant, the building is famous for its vast brick volume and the central tower which emphasises the horizontal mass. The building was decorated with terracotta detailing, stone cornices and arched windows, reflecting Venetian Gothic in industrial style. Closed after the Second World War and abandoned for decades, the complex underwent extensive renovation work at the beginning of the 21st century and was converted into a luxury hotel. The restoration project maintained the monumental nature of the original structure, introducing contemporary elements that emphasised the material solidity and historic value. Today, the Molino Stucky represents an example of converted industrial archaeology where architectural renovation has been able to return an iconic landmark to the city, maintaining the close links with its manufacturing past.

architects	**type**	**construction**
Ernst Wullekopf	multi-purpose	19th c.

56. Social Housing Complex in the Giudecca

Giudecca
30133 Venice

external viewing only

B > Hilton

This social housing complex in the Giudecca, designed between 1980 and 1986 by Gino Valle, represents one of the most interesting examples of 20th century residential architecture in Venice. Situated along the Fondamenta delle Zitelle, this project was built in a marginal area of the city, upgrading the zone through its architectural style with a combination of practicality and sensitivity to the Venetian environment. Valle organised the complex with a series of graduated buildings arranged around internal courtyards recalling traditional campielli. This choice does not simply create pleasant communal spaces but is also designed to subdivide the total building mass, adapting it to the sizes and proportions of the historic city. The facades are clad in exposed brick alternating with plastered sections, to establish a visual link with Venetian building traditions, but, at the same time, avoiding any form of imitation in style. The apartments, designed to satisfy all essential housing needs, are impressive for their light-filled and functional distribution. Attention to architectural detail, visible in the loggias and regular openings, provides the complex with an austere, but welcoming appearance. Valle's project fits smoothly into the context of civil architecture, able to combine the needs of modern lifestyle with a vision of urban and social quality.

© Jacqueline Poggi

architects
Gino Valle, Giorgio Micola

type
residential

construction
1980-1986

57. JW Marriott Resort & Spa

Isola Delle Rose
Laguna Di San Marco
30133 Venice

visits can be booked in advance

The JW Marriott Venice Resort & Spa, designed by Matteo Thun and opened in 2015, is a refined example of architectural renovation in the hospitality sector. Located on the Isola delle Rose, in the Venetian lagoon, the complex is integrated with a former 20th century health facility, now transformed into a luxury resort. The conversion project sensitively integrated contemporary design, taking care to respect the existing heritage buildings. Thun redesigned the spaces using a minimalist approach, focusing strongly on the relationship between architecture, landscape, and water. The intervention is based on natural materials like stone, wood and glass that communicate with the lush vegetation on the island. The private rooms and communal spaces were designed to maximise natural light, creating a relaxed harmonious atmosphere. The Spa centre is located on the rooftop and opens onto a panoramic pool with views over the lagoon, underlining the visual and perceptive link with Venice. The restoration maintained the building's original structure, introducing contemporary elements that highlight the formal simplicity through the "box-in-a-box" strategy. This project has been very successful in integrating environmental sustainability with restrained luxury, creating a resort which is an example of hospitality excellence in harmony with the lagoon.

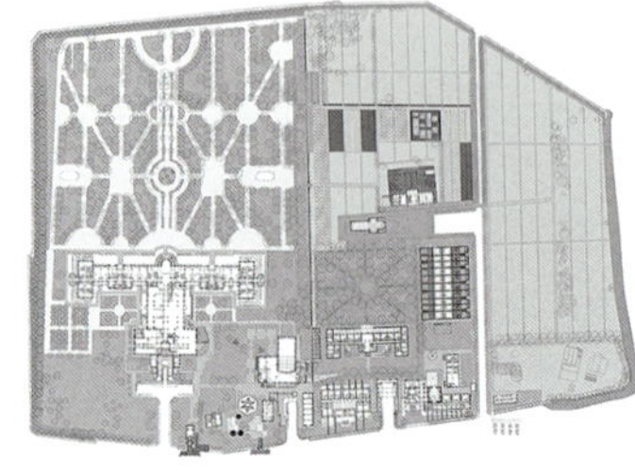

MatteoThun&Partners_JWMarriottVenice © JWMarriottVenice

architects
Matteo Thun & Partners

type
hospitality

construction
2015

58. Blue Moon Beach Resort

Piazza Bucintoro 1
30126 Lido VE

open to the public

1, 5.1, 5.2, 6, 10, 14, 20, N > Lido S.M.E.

The Blue Moon beach resort, designed by Giancarlo De Carlo in the 1960s, is a project that connects architecture and landscape, in response to the increasing needs of tourism on the Lido di Venezia. Designed in a modern functional style, the structure is composed of a series of horizontal buildings arranged parallel to the coastline to highlight the connection with the beach and the sea. The structure was designed to integrate with the natural environment without visibly imposing its presence through the careful choice of materials and proportions. The wide glazed surfaces provide visual continuity between interior and exterior while the lightweight roofing and exposed concrete give the structure a simple rational appearance. Internally, the space is designed to guarantee easy traffic flow, connecting the service areas with the relaxation zone, while maintaining the strong connection with the beach environment. The Blue Moon is a fine example of seaside resort architecture, able to respond to practical necessities while, at the same time, expressing sophisticated design based on a fine balance between form, function and landscape.

© Jacqueline Poggi

architects
Giancarlo De Carlo

type
commercial

construction
1995-2002

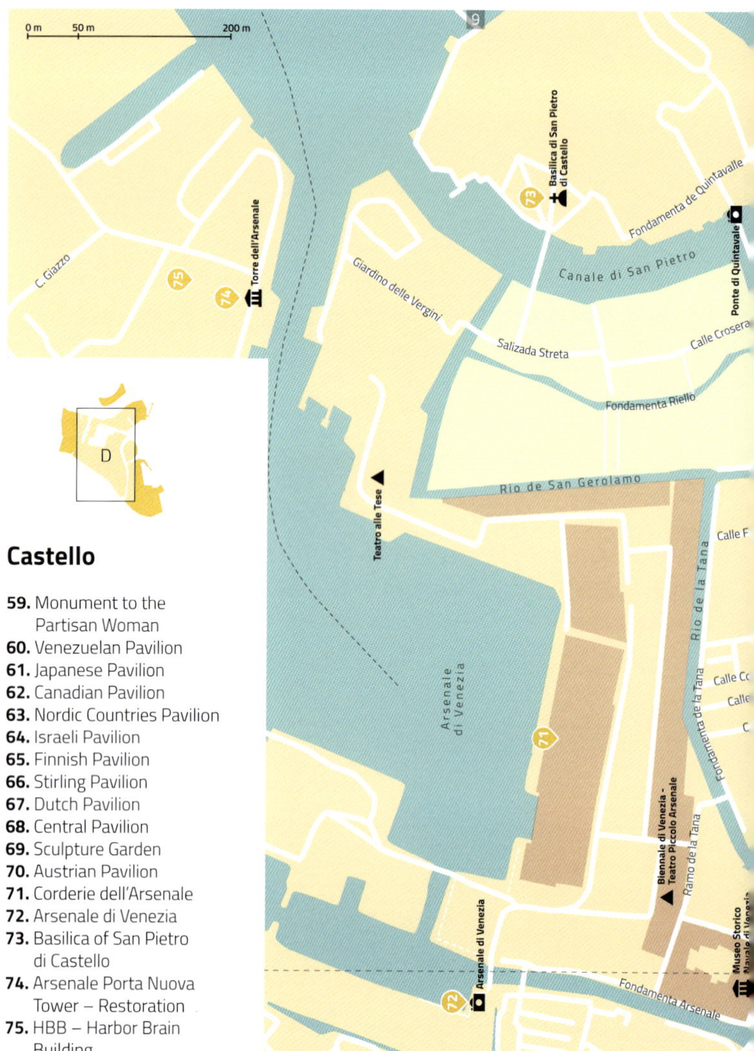

Castello

59. Monument to the Partisan Woman
60. Venezuelan Pavilion
61. Japanese Pavilion
62. Canadian Pavilion
63. Nordic Countries Pavilion
64. Israeli Pavilion
65. Finnish Pavilion
66. Stirling Pavilion
67. Dutch Pavilion
68. Central Pavilion
69. Sculpture Garden
70. Austrian Pavilion
71. Corderie dell'Arsenale
72. Arsenale di Venezia
73. Basilica of San Pietro di Castello
74. Arsenale Porta Nuova Tower – Restoration
75. HBB – Harbor Brain Building

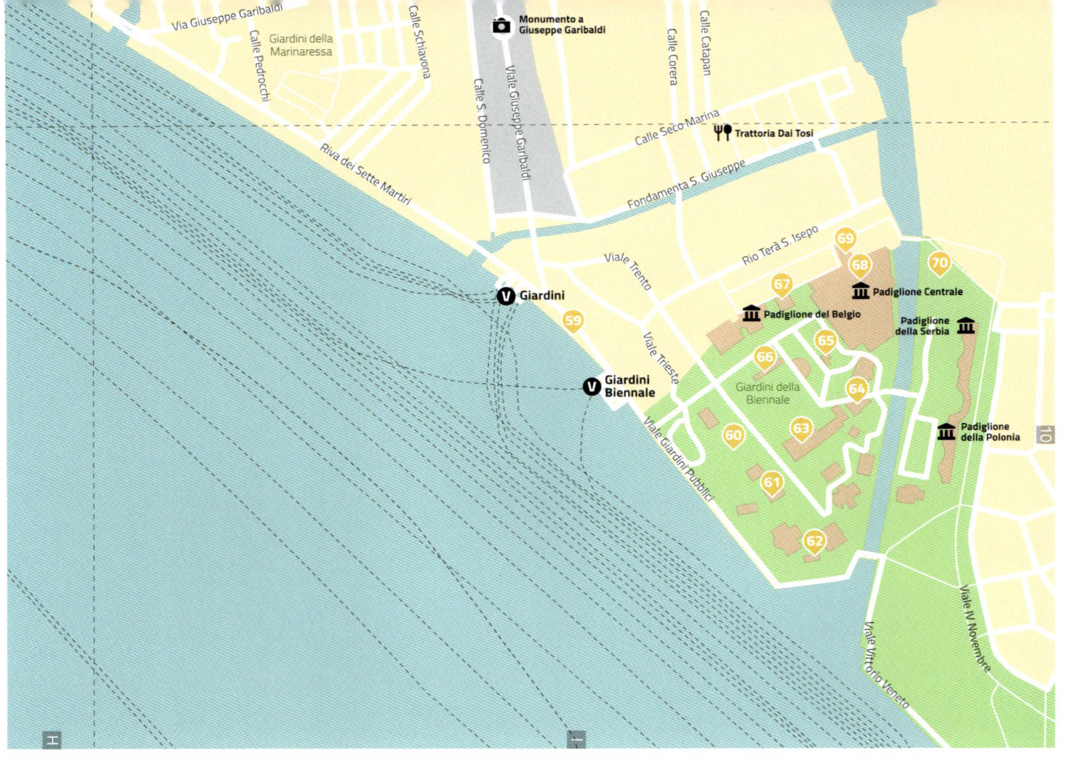
Via Giuseppe Garibaldi
Giardini della Marinaressa
Calle Pedrocchi
Calle Schiavona
Monumento a Giuseppe Garibaldi
Calle S. Domenico
Viale Giuseppe Garibaldi
Calle Corera
Calle Catapan
Calle Seco Marina
Trattoria Dai Tosi
Fondamenta S. Giuseppe
Riva dei Sette Martiri
Rio Terà S. Isepo
Viale Trento
Giardini
59
69
68
70
67
Padiglione Centrale
Padiglione del Belgio
Padiglione della Serbia
65
66
Viale Trieste
Giardini Biennale
Giardini della Biennale
64
60
63
Padiglione della Polonia
10
Viale Giardini Pubblici
61
62
Viale IV Novembre
Viale Vittorio Veneto
H
I

59. Monument to the Partisan Woman

Castello
30100 Venice

open to the public

1, 10, N > Giardini A
1, N > Giardini B
4.2, 5.2, 6 > Giardini Biennale A
4.1, 5.1, 6 > Giardini Biennale B

The Monument to the Partisan Woman, inaugurated in 1957, was originally composed of a base created by Carlo Scarpa, bearing a ceramic statue by the sculptor Leoncillo Leonardi. Later, as a result of a Neo-fascist aggression, the sculpture was destroyed and replaced with a new piece, following a competition held in 1969. The project was designed to honour the women of the Resistance and makes a powerful impact for its integration between architecture, sculpture and lagoon landscape. The monument is composed of a platform in original Istrian stone extending out into the water, creating a kind of threshold between land and sea. It supports the bronze sculpture by Augusto Murer, showing the body of a partisan woman, lying, almost floating on the surface of the water. The aquatic element is an integral part of the project, reflecting the sky and visually changing with the tides and light at different times of day. Scarpa designed a silent, contemplative monument; the symbolic value is expressed through the choice of materials and the relationship with its surroundings. The Monument to the Partisan Woman is a work with strongly evocative impact and is an example of how architecture can transmit the collective memory, creating a place for respectful reflection in the heart of the city.

© Valentina Spagnoli

architects
Carlo Scarpa

type
monument

construction
1957 / 1969

60. Venezuelan Pavilion

Giardini della Biennale
30100 Venice

visitable during La Biennale
+39 041 5218 711
info@labiennale.org
www.labiennale.org

1, 10, N > Giardini A
1, N > Giardini B
4.2, 5.2, 6 >
Giardini Biennale A
4.1, 5.1, 6 >
Giardini Biennale B

The Venezuelan Pavilion, created by Carlo Scarpa in 1956, is one of most refined examples of exhibition architecture in the Venetian Giardini della Biennale. The Pavilion is perfectly integrated in the surrounding landscape and is impressive for Scarpa's mastery in combining materials, light, and spatial geometry. The building is designed as a series of structures arranged around open spaces and fluid pathways, where the relationship between interior and exterior is always present. The pavilion is based on a sequence of rooms connected by open passageways and glazed openings that provide constant interaction with the vegetation and the natural light. The use of materials like concrete, wood and Istria stone give the building a refined tactile effect, completely coherent with Scarpa's design method. A great deal of attention was paid to construction details, like the slot lighting, and the jointing between different materials, that create dynamic effects in the space. The Venezuelan Pavilion is a project that reflects Scarpa's poetics, where the boundaries between architecture and nature merge in a perfect balance between form, materials and sensorial perception.

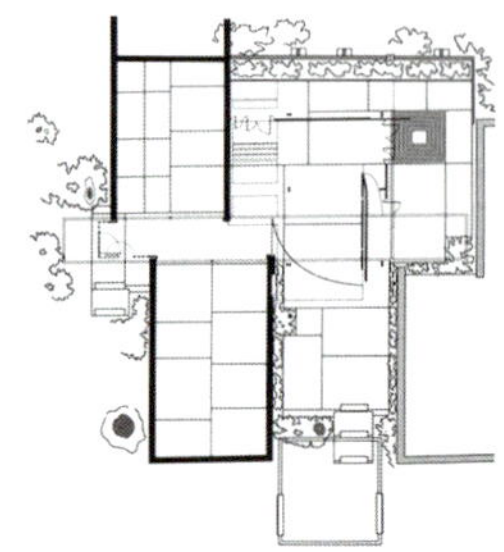

© Chiara Mezzabotta

architects
Carlo Scarpa

type
cultural

construction
1956

61. Japanese Pavilion

Giardini della Biennale
30100 Venice

visitable during La Biennale
+39 041 5218 711
info@labiennale.org
www.labiennale.org

1, 10, N > Giardini A
1, N > Giardini B
4.2, 5.2, 6 > Giardini Biennale A
4.1, 5.1, 6 > Giardini Biennale B

The Japanese Pavilion, designed by Takamasa Yoshizaka in 1956, is an emblematic example of the encounter between Western Modernism and traditional Japanese architecture. A student of Le Corbusier, Yoshizaka developed a design style that combined Rationalist principles with elements typical of Japanese building culture, with a strong focus on lightweight structure and close contact with nature. The pavilion features an open plan layout, built mainly of wood and concrete, materials that define the pared-back, but strongly evocative design. The wooden beam system and slender columns give the impression of a building suspended in space, while the glazed surfaces provide constant interaction between interior and exterior. The internal layout follows the principles of exhibition space flexibility, with special attention to natural light which filters through carefully calibrated openings to create a contemplative atmosphere. The Japanese Pavilion represents a model of integration between architecture and landscape, maintaining a perfect balance between innovation and memory, lightweight construction and spatial depth.

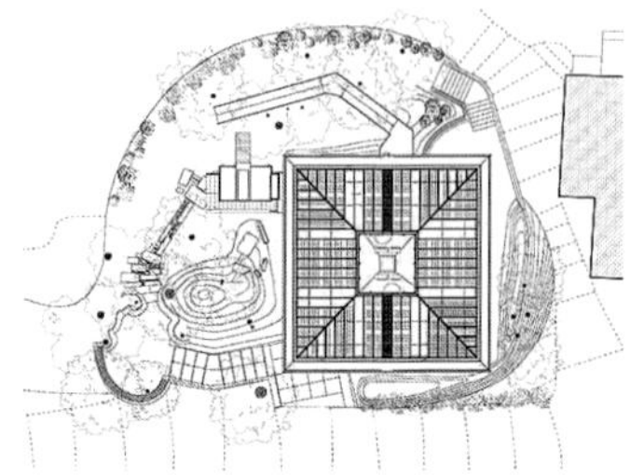

© Chiara Mezzabotta

architects
Takamasa Yoshizaka

type
cultural

construction
1956

62. Canadian Pavilion

Giardini della Biennale
30100 Venice

visitable during La Biennale
+39 041 5218 711
info@labiennale.org
www.labiennale.org

1, 10, N > Giardini A
1, N > Giardini B
4.2, 5.2, 6 > Giardini Biennale A
4.1, 5.1, 6 > Giardini Biennale B

The Canadian Pavilion, designed by the Milanese firm BBPR in 1958, is a structure based on the Rationalist style, but where special care was taken to integrate the building into the landscape of the Giardini della Biennale in Venice. The project features a geometrical composition and an innovative use of light and construction materials. The pavilion is built around a central element encircled by a staggered, overhanging roof, providing protective shade and highlighting the continuity between interior and exterior. The brick and concrete walls are topped by large glazed windows providing views of the surrounding vegetation. The interior has been organised for maximum flexibility, where modules are used to separate exhibition spaces; a continuous circuit guides visitors through the various sections of the exhibition. The architectural style of the Canadian Pavilion demonstrates how BBPR was able to combine Modernist rigour with a sensitivity to the surrounding environment, creating a building that is harmoniously integrated within the Biennale landscape. The construction quality and choice of materials give the pavilion a distinctive character, making it one of the most interesting architectural examples in the Biennale gardens.

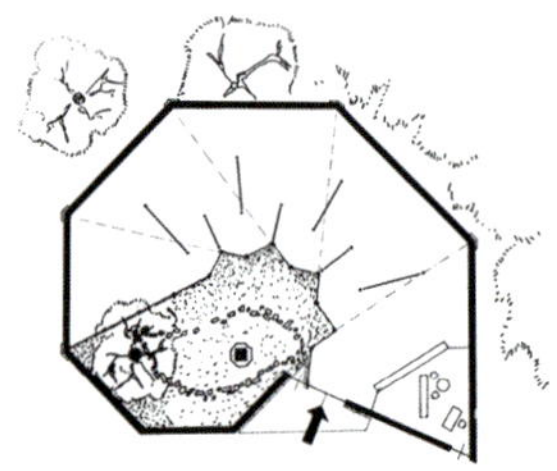

© Valentina Spagnoli

architects	**type**	**construction**
Gruppo BBPR	cultural	1958

63. Nordic Countries Pavilion

Giardini della Biennale
30100 Venice

visitable during La Biennale
+39 041 5218 711
info@labiennale.org
www.labiennale.org

1, 10, N > Giardini A
1, N > Giardini B
4.2, 5.2, 6 > Giardini Biennale A
4.1, 5.1, 6 > Giardini Biennale B

The Nordic Countries Pavilion, designed by Sverre Fehn and inaugurated in 1962, is one of the most remarkable projects of the Venice Biennale for its close relationship with nature and its refined fusion of Modernism and Nordic sensibility. The structure was integrated within the Giardini della Biennale environment with extreme care, paying close attention to include the existing trees as an integral part of the project. The building is composed of a system of raw concrete partitions and vast glazed surfaces to create a space that is very sober but full of light. The roof consists of a double layer of crossed beams, covered with an undulated fibreglass brise-soleil: diffused natural light filters through to create a dynamic, ever-changing atmosphere during the day. Fehn designed the pavilion as a structure in a constant relationship with nature, where several trees grow up physically through the constructed space and roof. This approach reflects the Nordic way of life, where the relationship with the environment is a fundamental element in project design. The Nordic Countries Pavilion is a masterpiece in its perfect balance of construction and landscape, Rational design and poetic sensitivity.

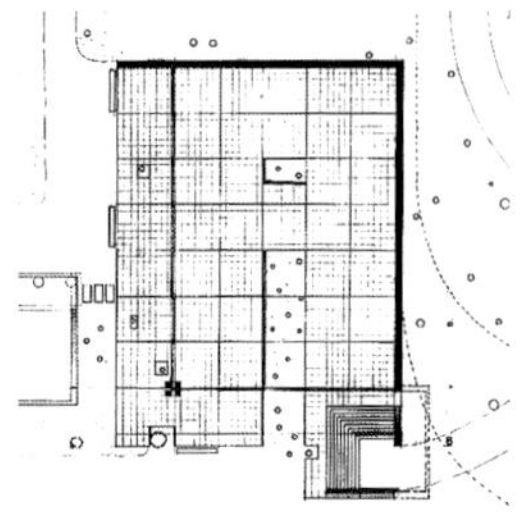

architects	**type**	**construction**
Sverre Fehn	cultural	1962

64. Israeli Pavilion

Campo Giazzo,
Giardini della Biennale
30100 Venice

visitable during La Biennale
+39 041 5218 711
info@labiennale.org
www.labiennale.org

1, 10, N > Giardini A
1, N > Giardini B
4.2, 5.2, 6 >
Giardini Biennale A
4.1, 5.1, 6 >
Giardini Biennale B

The Israeli Pavilion, designed by Zeev Rechter and inaugurated in 1952, is one of the most unequivocal expressions of international Modernism applied to exhibition architecture. Rechter, a key figure in 20th century Israeli architecture, designed a building that is a blend of Rationalist principles with a Mediterranean influence, perfectly adapted to the climate and light of Venice. The pavilion is based on an open layout with a clever use of natural light filtered through the large glazed surfaces, creating a balance between solidity and transparency. The white walls and simple design emphasise the geometrical purity of the composition, while the gently sloping roof modifies the perception of the space. The internal layout answers exhibition display needs with an architectural concept that does not impose any particular interpretation, but leaves artists and curators with maximum freedom of expression. The Israeli Pavilion demonstrates its capacity to be a neutral exhibition space and an iconic piece of architecture at the same time, where light and straightforward design are the primary elements.

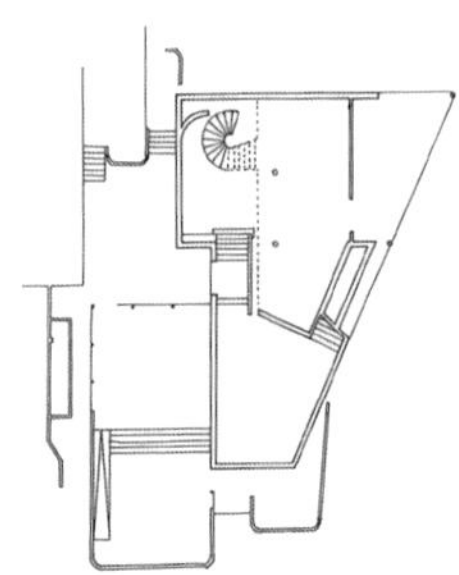

© Chiara Mezzabotta

architects	**type**	**construction**
Zeev Rechter	cultural	1952

65. Finnish Pavilion

Giardini della Biennale
30100 Venice

visitable during La Biennale
+39 041 5218 711
info@labiennale.org
www.labiennale.org

1, 10, N > Giardini A
1, N > Giardini B
4.2, 5.2, 6 >
Giardini Biennale A
4.1, 5.1, 6 >
Giardini Biennale B

The Finnish Pavilion designed by Alvar Aalto in 1956, is one of the most representative works of the Finnish architect's organic approach. Conceived as a temporary structure, the pavilion was later maintained thanks to the quality of its spatial concept and its perfect harmony within the Giardini della Biennale environment. The building was unusual for its innovative use of wood, emblematic material for Nordic architecture, used for the bearing structure as well as the internal cladding. The walls made from curved wooden panels create an impression of movement, and provide special acoustic effects, accentuating the relationship between space and sensorial perception. The slightly recessed entrance leads to a quiet enveloping space where natural light is filtered through carefully calculated openings, creating an intimate and contemplative atmosphere. Aalto designed the pavilion as a dynamic environment, able to adapt to a variety of exhibition requirements without losing its identity and individual architectural style. Lightweight materials and structural simplicity have made this pavilion a quintessential example of Scandinavian design applied to exhibition architecture, where functional aspects and aesthetics come together in perfect equilibrium.

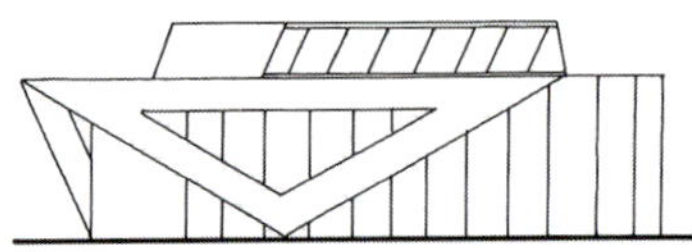

architects
Alvar Aalto

type
cultural

construction
1956

66. Stirling Pavilion

Giardini della Biennale
30100 Venice

visitable during La Biennale
+39 041 5218 711
info@labiennale.org
www.labiennale.org

1, 10, N > Giardini A
1, N > Giardini B
4.2, 5.2, 6 >
Giardini Biennale A
4.1, 5.1, 6 >
Giardini Biennale B

The Stirling Pavilion, designed by James Stirling in 1991, is one of the most interesting projects in the Giardini della Biennale in Venice. The pavilion, completed after Stirling's death by Michael Wilford, expresses the principles of Stirling's architectural style, where the relationship between form, function and context is represented in an expressive and experimental manner. The building is based on a complex layout, with a system of intersecting geometrical sections that define the dynamic exhibition space. The pavilion has a red brick facade interrupted by large glazed openings that establish a direct connection between interior and exterior. The sculptural roof jointing recalls industrial architecture and the hi-tech approach, typical of Stirling's work. The interior is designed to provide an immersive exhibition experience, with flexible spaces and careful attention to natural light variation. The attentive choice of materials and finishings contributes towards creating an atmosphere where the balance between tradition and innovation becomes the fundamental design element. Today, the Stirling Pavilion is a model for contemporary architectural research, an attestation to the architect's capacity to combine experimentation with historical heritage.

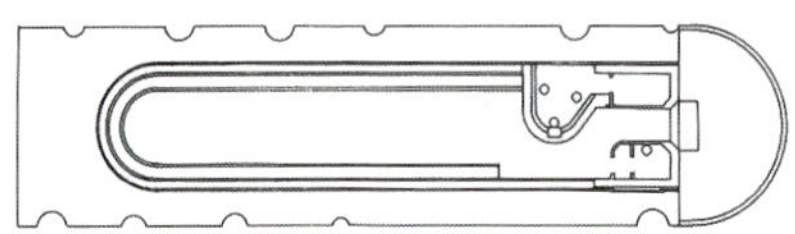

Courtesy of Archweb.com

architects
James Stirling

type
cultural

construction
1991

67. Dutch Pavilion

Calle Dietro Il Paludo 859,
Giardini della Biennale
30122 Venice

visitable during La Biennale
+39 041 5218 711
info@labiennale.org
www.labiennale.org

1, 10, N > Giardini A
1, N > Giardini B
4.2, 5.2, 6 > Giardini Biennale A
4.1, 5.1, 6 > Giardini Biennale B

The Dutch Pavilion, designed by Gerrit Thomas Rietveld and inaugurated in 1954 in the Giardini della Biennale, is an iconic model of Rationalist Modernism applied to exhibition architecture. Rietveld, a master of the De Stijl movement, designed the pavilion as a very simple building where the space was divided in strictly modular form and with a skilful use of natural light. The pavilion is based on an open plan layout, in a sequence of spaces without any visual barriers to accentuate the principle of spatial continuity. White surfaces and glazed panels create a subtle but luminous atmosphere in perfect harmony with the principles of Neoplasticism. The raised flooring and slender metal columns give the structure a lightweight effect, while the opening and closing systems provide constant communication between the interior and exterior. The pavilion's flexible design can be adapted for temporary exhibitions without affecting the permanent works on show. Rietveld's project perfectly embodies the ideal of architecture designed in the service of art, confirming that Modernist design can be perfectly integrated even in a contemporary context.

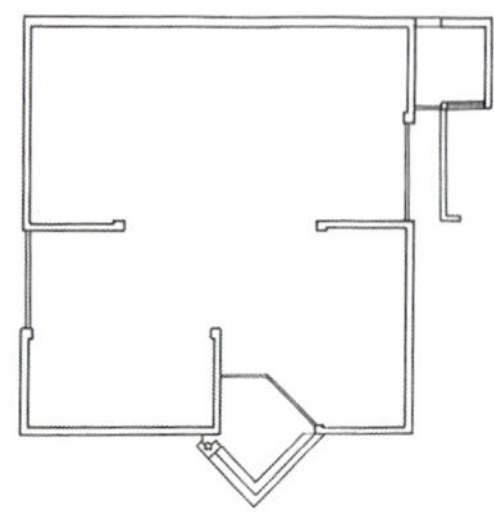

© Jacqueline Poggi

architects
Gerrit Thomas Rietveld

type
cultural

construction
1954

68. Central Pavilion

Calle Dietro Il Paludo 849,
Giardini della Biennale
30122 Venice

visitable during La Biennale
+39 041 5218 711
info@labiennale.org
www.labiennale.org

1, 10, N > Giardini A
1, N > Giardini B
4.2, 5.2, 6 > Giardini Biennale A
4.1, 5.1, 6 > Giardini Biennale B

The Central Pavilion, located in the Giardini della Biennale, represents the cornerstone of the internationally famous art and architecture exhibition. Originally designed in 1894 as the Italian Pavilion, the building underwent several changes and extensions during the 20th century, evolving to finally become the heart of the exhibition event. The pavilion design is a combination of Classical and Modern elements, with a symmetrical structure dominated by a large entrance staircase and a facade featuring a monumental portico. The architectural style shows a Rationalist influence, visible in the clean lines and plain geometry of the interior spaces. The large central nave, lit by overhead skylights, was designed to host temporary exhibitions, with modular partitions and flexible routes that permit a new interpretation of the space each time. During the various editions of the Biennale, the Central Pavilion has hosted some of the most important exhibitions of contemporary art and architecture, confirming its role as a reference point for artistic experimentation. The apparently neutral, but extremely versatile architectural design makes it one of the main exhibition resources of the Biennale, where the interaction between art works, space and the public is always constantly in progress.

architects
Enrico Trevisanato, Ernesto Basile, Gio Ponti, Carlo Scarpa, Valeriano Pastor, Massimo Bartolini, Rirkrit Tiravanija, Tobias Rehberger

type
cultural

construction
19th-20th sec.

69. Sculpture Garden

Padiglione Centrale
30122 Venice

visitable during La Biennale
+39 041 5218 711
info@labiennale.org
www.labiennale.org

1, 10, N > Giardini A
1, N > Giardini B
4.2, 5.2, 6 >
Giardini Biennale A
4.1, 5.1, 6 >
Giardini Biennale B

The Sculpture Garden, one of Carlo Scarpa's most emblematic projects, is located behind the Central Pavilion in the Giardini della Biennale, and represents a fundamental milestone in Italy's approach to open air museums. The garden was created to host a selection of sculptures in a space specifically designed to establish a close relationship between art, the architectural context and nature. The garden is small in scale, but divided into various sections; Scarpa designed it as a system of various levels and thresholds, where materials, vegetation and light combine in an immersive and calibrated setting. Water pools, polished stone surfaces, burnished metal inserts, and cast-in-place concrete are combined with the usual precision and refined taste for which he is famous. The garden appears as a micro-architecture through which the visitor is guided along a measured route composed of fleeting glimpses, pauses and walkways, designed to frame the sculptures and to stimulate a gradual perception of the space. The sculptures, often positioned on specifically designed bases, do not impose their presence individually, but are part of a dialogue with the terrain, surrounding walls, water features and pathways passing through the pavilion. Still today, the garden has maintained its fascinating atmosphere as a suspended and transitional space: a place where art and architecture interact with the sensitivity, details, setting, and deep relationship with time and the surroundings.

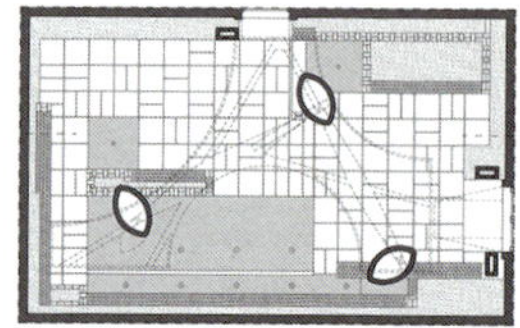

architects
Carlo Scarpa

type
cultural

construction
1952

70. Austrian Pavilion

Giardini della Biennale
30100 Venice

visitable during La Biennale
+39 041 5218 711
info@labiennale.org
www.labiennale.org

1, 10, N > Giardini A
1, N > Giardini B
4.2, 5.2, 6 >
Giardini Biennale A
4.1, 5.1, 6 >
Giardini Biennale B

The Austrian Pavilion was designed by Josef Hoffmann for the Giardini della Biennale in Venice in 1934, and represents an important example of Middle European Rationalist architecture. A central figure of the Wiener Werkstätte and Modernist Austrian architecture, Hoffmann designed a rectangular building in a very simple geometrical style, without any superfluous decoration. The distinctive element of the pavilion is its rhythmic facade punctuated by a series of white pillars that add a dynamic and deeper effect. A measured use of natural light enters through large openings, providing a connection between interior and exterior. The internal spaces were designed to guarantee great exhibition flexibility, accentuating the neutral architecture as an ideal background for displaying art works. In this project, Hoffmann applied the principles of Viennese Modernism, with a structure that combines formal clarity and functionality. The inclusion of this pavilion in the Biennale context makes it one of the most interesting examples of how Rationalist design was able to cater to the needs of exhibition spaces, without losing any of its autonomous and iconic architectural style.

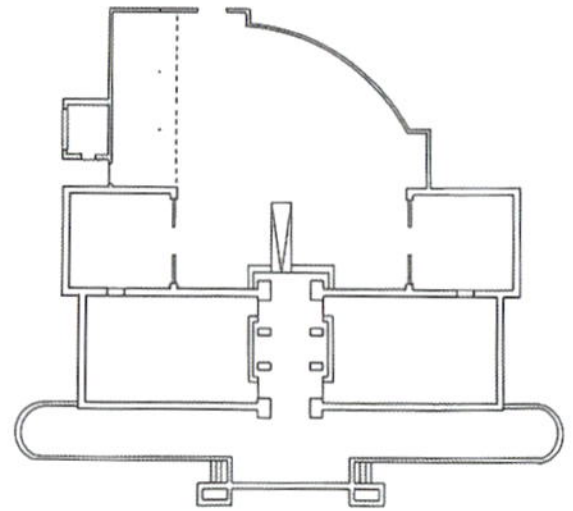

architects
Josef Hoffmann

type
cultural

construction
1934

71. Corderie dell'Arsenale

Campo de la Tana 2169
30122 Venice

visitable during La Biennale
+39 041 5218 711
info@labiennale.org
www.comune.venezia.it/it/arsenaledivenezia

1, 4.1, 4.2, B > Arsenale
4.1, 4.2, 5.1, 5.2, 22, B > Bacini – Arsenale Nord

The Corderie dell'Arsenale, built in 1303 under the Venetian Republic, is one of the most imposing demonstrations of Venetian industrial architecture. Originally destined for the production of hawsers for the Venetian navy, the Corderie forms a large building, over 300 metres long, supported by a series of brick pillars. The architectural design of the Corderie is a fine example of Medieval rational construction, with modular spaces and a massive, regular bearing structure. The monumental setting is emphasised by the light which enters through the side openings. Now transformed into a large exhibition space for contemporary art and architecture, today the Corderie hosts events and exhibitions during the Biennale. The quality of the construction materials and the expressive strength of the building were maintained intact during the renovations, confirming the capacity of historical industrial architecture to adapt, providing spaces for new purposes without losing any of the original character.

© Rodolfo Moro Courtesy Antica Corderia Verona

architects	**type**	**construction**
-	cultural	1303

72. Arsenale di Venezia

Campo de la Tana 2169
30122 Venice

visitable during La Biennale
+39 041 5218 711
info@labiennale.org
www.comune.venezia.it/it/arsenaledivenezia

1, 4.1, 4.2, B > Arsenale
4.1, 4.2, 5.1, 5.2, 22, B > Bacini – Arsenale Nord

The Arsenale di Venezia (dockyards and workshops) is one of the most imposing industrial complexes in history, a symbol of the naval power of the Venetian Republic (Serenissima) and a trailblazer for modern assembly line production. Founded in 1104 and extended over the following centuries, the Arsenale covers an area of almost 120 acres, surrounded by massive walls that guaranteed construction secrets and protection. This vast dockyard became the hub of Venetian galley ship construction, based on production methods and technology that were revolutionary for the period. As part of the urban plan, the Arsenale was built around a system of wet docks and internal canals designed to facilitate extremely efficient ship assembly and transport. Even as early as the 16th century, Venice used a mass production method able to build a galley ship in less than a day, an innovation which was centuries ahead of the modern Ford Motor production lines. As well as its military function, the Arsenale had a central role in the expansion of Venice, contributing to the economic and social growth of the city. Today, part of the complex is destined for the Biennale, with exhibition spaces created within some of the ancient structures in a fascinating dialogue between industrial archaeology and contemporary art. Its transformation as a cultural hub demonstrates the capacity of the city to reinterpret its historical heritage in an innovative manner, while maintaining the memory of its glorious naval history alive.

architects	**type**	**construction**
-	multi-purpose	1104

73. Basilica of San Pietro di Castello

S. Pietro di Castello
30122 Venice

Mon - Sat / 10.30 am - 5 pm
+39 041 2750 462
info@chorusvenezia.org
www.chorusvenezia.org

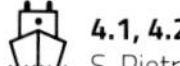 **4.1, 4.2, 5.1, 5.2** >
S. Pietro di Castello

The Basilica of San Pietro di Castello, located on the island of the same name, and seat of the Patriarchy of Venice until 1807, is an important example of Venetian Renaissance architecture. The construction was begun in the 15th century by Mauro Codussi and completed by Andrea Palladio in the latter half of the 16th century. He created the facade and the interior layout of the church. The basilica's architecture combines elements of Gothic and classical Renaissance styles. The monumental effect of the Istria stone facade is created by a tympanum supported by Corinthian pillars designed with geometrical sobriety. The interior has a single nave with side chapels, and is divided by rounded arches. The Palladian sense of space is emphasised by the light that enters through the Diocletian windows. The dome is the central element of the composition, emerging from the tall drum and dominating the profile of the church, creating a graceful vertical effect. The Basilica of San Pietro di Castello represents a fundamental passage in the evolution of Venetian religious architecture marking the transition from Gothic to classical Renaissance, and paying homage to two of the most illustrious architects of the Venetian Republic (Serenissima).

© Godromil

architects
Mauro Codussi,
Andrea Palladio

type
religious

construction
15th-16th c.

74. Arsenale Porta Nuova Tower – Restoration

Salizada Streta 98
30122 Venice

Mon - Fri / 8 am - 3 pm

1, 4.1, 4.2, B > Arsenale
4.1, 4.2, 5.1, 5.2 > S. Pietro di Castello

The restoration project for the Arsenale Porta Nuova Tower, designed by MAP studio, is a fine example of Venetian industrial and military heritage building renovation. The building, built in the 19th century as part of the Arsenale complex, remained in a state of neglect for a long period, up until the recent renovation project which restored its purpose through careful consolidation and redevelopment work. The project is based on an approach that respected the historic identity of the tower, with interventions aimed at preserving the original structure and internal layout. The brick and metal structural elements were restored and highlighted, while the introduction of new technological solutions enabled the building to be adapted to modern requirements. The interior was redesigned to host cultural and exhibition spaces, maintaining a constant dialogue between past and present. The Porta Nuova Tower renovation is part of a wider urban renewal process at the Arsenale, confirming the importance of the conservation projects currently underway to preserve Venetian heritage buildings. The MAP studio project is an excellent restoration model that combines respect for existing buildings while upgrading them for new purposes, restoring a fragment of the city's past with a vision towards the future.

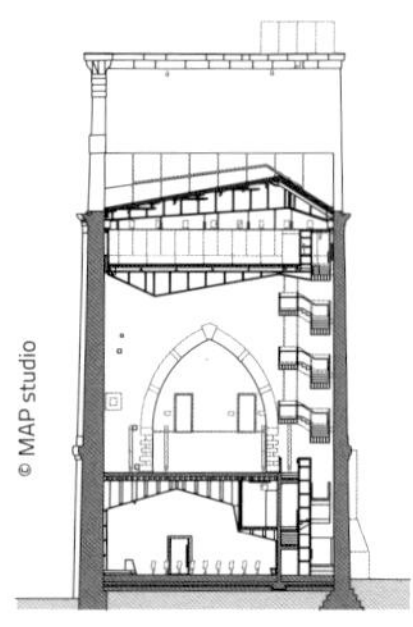

© MAP studio

© Alessandra Chemollo. Courtesy MAP studio

architects
MAP studio

type
public space

construction
2011

75. HBB – Harbor Brain Building

Campo Giazzo
30122 Venice

by appointment
info@consorziovenezianuova.com

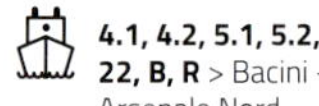
4.1, 4.2, 5.1, 5.2, 22, B, R > Bacini - Arsenale Nord

The Harbor Brain Building, designed by C+S Architects, represents one of the projects in the recent Venice Arsenale renewal plans. The building is in a historical and industrial logistics context, currently undergoing renovation for conversion to an innovative research and technology hub. The project is interesting for its austere architectural style based on rigorous calculations involving the proportions and the use of industrial materials reinterpreted in contemporary style. The structure is composed of a compact volume, defined by a modular facade with alternating glazed surfaces and opaque panels that create a dynamic rhythm and constant interaction with natural light. The interiors are designed to provide spatial flexibility where spaces are organised for co-working and interdisciplinary collaboration. There has been a strong focus on sustainability, with natural ventilation systems, solar panels, and energy saving solutions. The integration of the Harbor Brain Building within the urban fabric is an excellent example of restoration in the naval area, confirming the capacity of contemporary architecture to cohabit with the past without sacrificing innovation. This project by C+S Architects is an example of a clever balance between function, aesthetics, and sustainability, redefining the concept of productive space in urban Venice.

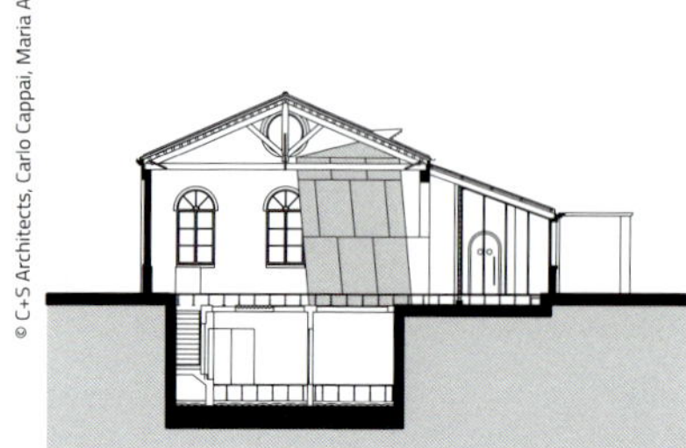

architects
C+S Architects

type
public space

construction
2011

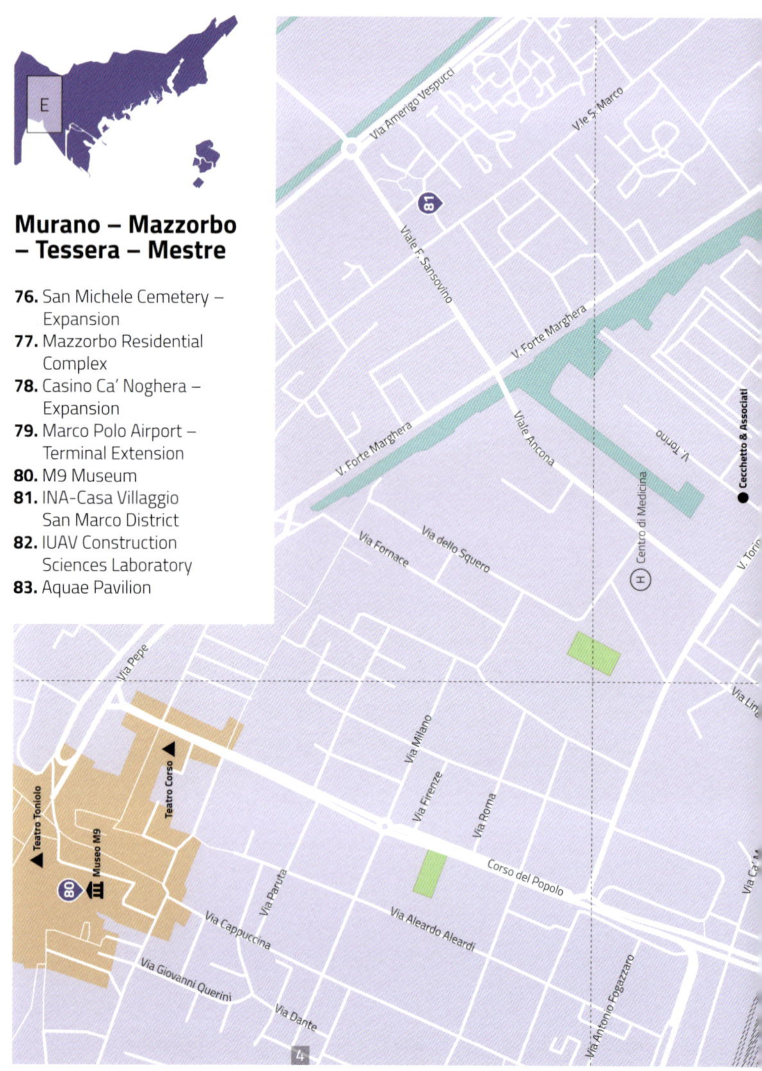

Murano – Mazzorbo – Tessera – Mestre

76. San Michele Cemetery – Expansion
77. Mazzorbo Residential Complex
78. Casino Ca' Noghera – Expansion
79. Marco Polo Airport – Terminal Extension
80. M9 Museum
81. INA-Casa Villaggio San Marco District
82. IUAV Construction Sciences Laboratory
83. Aquae Pavilion

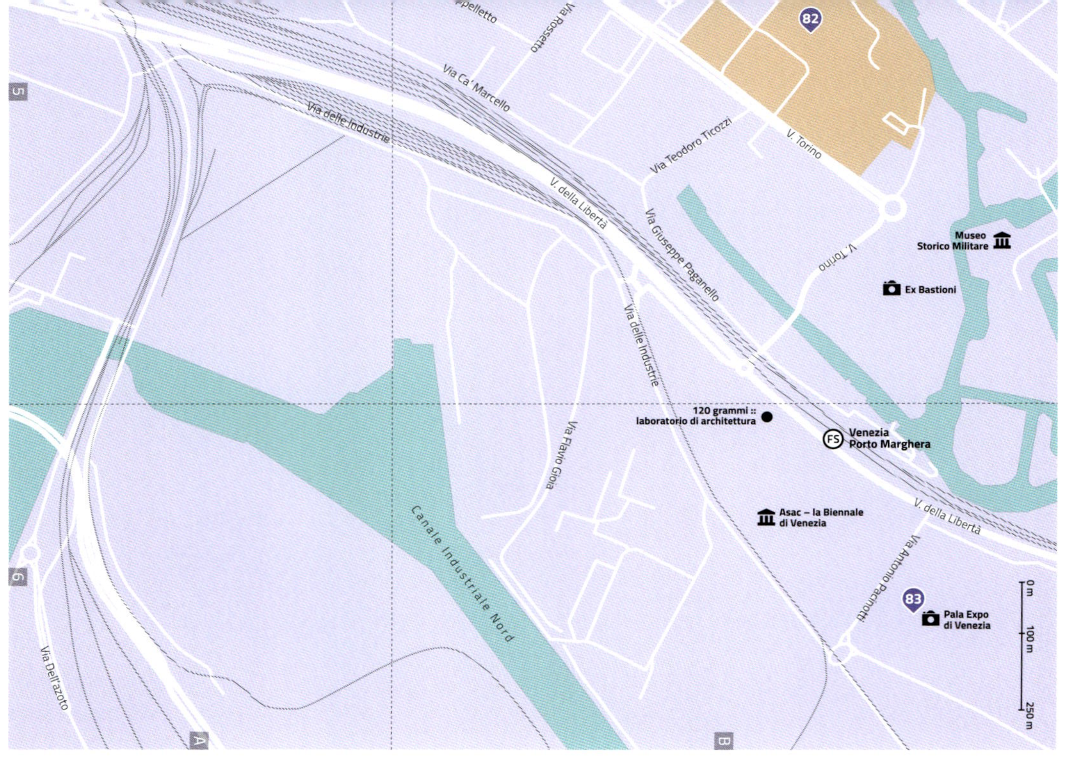

82
Via Rossetto
Via Ca' Marcello
Via delle Industrie
Via Teodoro Ticozzi
V. Torino
V. della Libertà
Via Giuseppe Paganello
V. Torino
Museo
Storico Militare
Ex Bastioni
Via delle Industrie
120 grammi ::
laboratorio di architettura
FS
Venezia
Porto Marghera
Via Flavio Gioia
Asac – la Biennale
di Venezia
V. della Libertà
Canale Industriale Nord
Via Antonio Pacinotti
83
Pala Expo
di Venezia
0 m
100 m
250 m
Via Dell'azoto
5
6
A
B

76. San Michele Cemetery – Expansion

Isola di San Michele
30121 Venice

Mon - Sun / 7.30 am - 6 pm
+39 041 9655 525

www.comune.venezia.it/it/content/cimitero-smichele

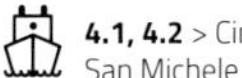
4.1, 4.2 > Cimitero San Michele

The San Michele cemetery expansion, designed by David Chipperfield Architects London and Milan and completed in 2017, is a blend of rigorous composition and spiritual sensitivity: a reinterpretation of the traditional cemetery in contemporary form. Located on the San Michele burial island, the project was designed as a series of courtyards and colonnades to create a dialogue between architecture and the landscape. The layout is based on a geometrical grid to create open and enclosed spaces in a regular, meditative sequence. The architect chose dark gray exposed concrete and white Istria stone to emphasise the silent austerity of the cemetery, evoking a spiritual atmosphere that is both secular and universal. Natural light, filtered through openings and secluded spaces, helps to create an atmosphere of reflection. This project was not created simply as a functional extension, but also as a reflection on the meaning of the cemetery, conceived as a space for remembrance and contemplation. Chipperfield created a deep connection with the city, demonstrating how contemporary architecture can interpret universal topics while maintaining close bonds with the specific site.

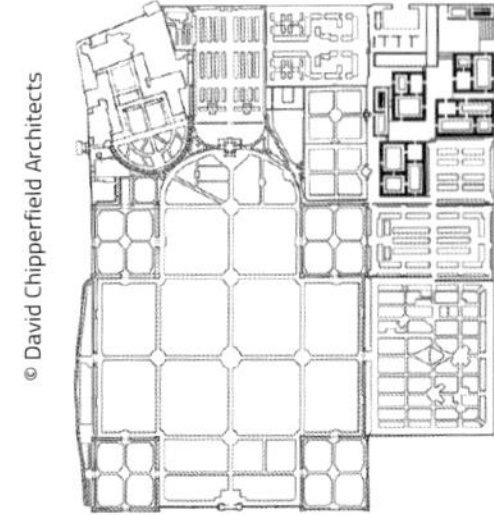
© David Chipperfield Architects

© Alessandra Chemollo. Courtesy David Chipperfield Architects

architects
David Chipperfield Architects
London and Milan

type
cemetery

construction
2017

77. Mazzorbo Residential Complex

Calle Larga Bassan 101
30142 Venice

external viewing only

 **12, NLN** > Mazzorbo

The Mazzorbo residential complex, designed by Giancarlo De Carlo, represents one of the most accomplished expressions of his architectural vision, based on a dialogue with the local context and the active participation of its inhabitants. The project proposes an alternative residential building model, able to combine environmental sustainability and well-rooted integration in the territory. The layout is based on a courtyard structure, unlike the typical rigidly standardised style of mid 20th century buildings. De Carlo proposes a dynamic and well-structured layout, where the different volumes create fluid circulation paths as well as private and semi-public spaces. The use of local materials, such as exposed brick, wood and coloured plasterwork, reinforces the bond with the local district enhancing its characteristic aspects. Special care was taken to link the interior and exterior: door and window openings are arranged in unconventional positions, and loggias and terraces provide evocative glimpses of the lagoon. The project is also outstanding for its environmental sensitivity: the existing vegetation was preserved and integrated into the urban layout, and the orientation of the buildings provides maximum natural light and ventilation. With this project, De Carlo has once again demonstrated how architecture can contribute towards creating spaces that cater to the actual needs of the inhabitants, while interacting with the local territory with respect and awareness.

architects
Giancarlo De Carlo

type
residential

construction
1980-1997

78. Casino Ca' Noghera – Expansion

Via Paliaga 4/8
30173 Venice

open to the public
+39 041 5297 111

www.casinovenezia.it/it/sedi/canoghera

45, 45H >
Ca' Noghera Casinò
4, 8, 10, 25, 29 >
Ca' Noghera

The expansion of the Venice Ca' Noghera Casino was designed by architects, Enrico Dusi and Matteo Ghidoni. The project involved the redevelopment and extension of the gambling and entertainment structure. Located on the Venetian mainland, it was the first example of an American-style casino in Italy, featuring open flexible spaces designed to host a wide range of gambling and entertainment activities. The expansion project was aimed at two objectives: to increase the capacity of the structure and to redefine the architectural style of the complex, creating a stronger, more distinctive identity. The intervention resulted in the creation of new gaming rooms, a lounge area, restaurants, and spaces destined for events and entertainment, thus providing a multifunctional environment to attract a diversified public. The new expanded layout is composed of a modular system of geometrical spaces arranged in a sequence that underlines the continuity with the surrounding landscape. Large glazed expanses provide views connecting the interior and exterior, reducing the usual sense of enclosure typical of gambling structures. Natural light is filtered through metal screens with dynamic patterns, creating a sophisticated but welcoming atmosphere, unlike the familiar artificial and overstimulating lighting normally found in conventional casinos.

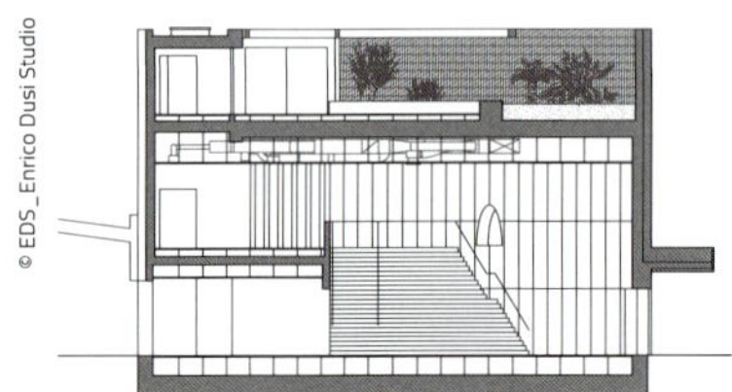

© EDS_Enrico Dusi Studio

architects
Enrico Dusi Studio,
Matteo Ghidoni

type
commercial

construction
2021

79. Marco Polo Airport – Terminal Extension

Viale Galileo Galilei 30
30173 Venice

open to the public

www.veneziaairport.it

45, 45H > Triestina Zorzi, Triestina Zuliani

The extension and re-designing of the Marco Polo Airport passenger terminal represents two of the most important infrastructural projects in the Venetian area. Designed by One Works, the intervention is part of a strategic plan to deal with the increase in air traffic, plus improving operational efficiency and providing a more welcoming passenger area. The first part, inaugurated in 2017, extended the existing structure by about 11,000 square metres, creating a new forecourt: a gallery 280 metres long and 22 metres wide, forming a filter between the city, the terminal and transport systems. This space was obtained by re-purposing the area between the original building and the overhead roadway, creating a continuous light-filled environment. A striking feature is the large undulating steel and glass roof that filters natural light into the departure and arrival levels, improving environmental comfort and enhancing the architectural design. The rational internal distribution flow is connected with the Water Terminal, the docks, the multi-level car park, and the roofed pedestrian traffic areas, including the moving walkway. The stone, wood and metal construction recalls traditional local building materials and helps to root the project within the Venetian context. The expansion project continues with new areas under construction to the north-east, and with further development planned towards the south-west, both part of the long-term master plan.

© One Works

© Alessandra Chemollo. Courtesy One Works

architects
One Works

type
infrastructure

construction
2017

80. M9 Museum

Via Giovanni Pascoli 11
30171 Venice

Wed - Fri / 10 am - 6 pm
Sat - Sun / 10 am - 7 pm
+39 041 0995 941
info@m9museum.it
www.m9museum.it

8/, 9E, 9S, 10, 10S, 13, 16, 21, 31, 45, 53, N1 > Olivi
3, 7, 7E, 7L, 8AE, 8E, 9S, 10, 10S, 12E, 13, 16, 21, 31, 45, 53, N1 > Carducci Pascoli

The M9 Museum, designed by Sauerbruch Hutton and inaugurated in Mestre in 2018, is one of the most ambitious urban renewal operations created in the Venetian area. Integrated within a widely transformed historical-industrial context, the museum attracts immediate attention for its innovative use of materials and architectural style which combines sustainability and technology. The compact but irregular building appears as a dynamic monolith clad in a mosaic of vibrant ceramic panels that reflect the colours of Venice and create an iridescent effect according to the light. Ceramic materials were used not only for their aesthetics, but also for their functional action as climate control for the building. The interior is spread over several floors, offering flexible exhibition spaces, and is equipped with advanced technology to create immersive interaction with multimedia content. The large entrance hall was designed as a covered urban piazza, a meeting place to create a relationship between the museum and the city. The Sauerbruch Hutton project represents an effective example of how contemporary architecture can interact with historic contexts without indulging in imitation, redefining the role of new cultural buildings within urban environments.

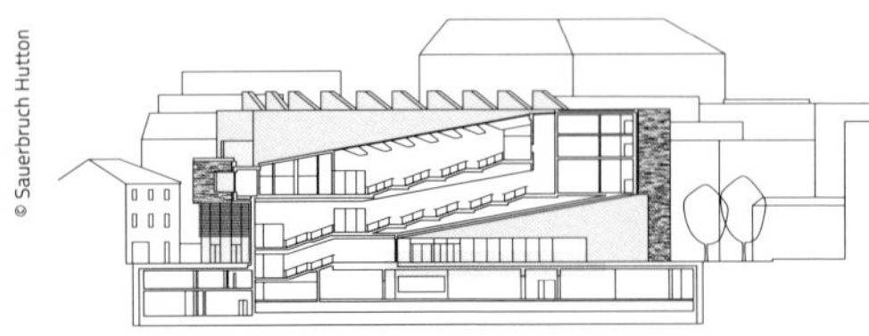

© Jan Bitter. Courtesy Sauerbruch Hutton

architects
Sauerbruch Hutton

type
cultural

construction
2018

81. INA-Casa Villaggio San Marco District

Viale S. Marco
30173 Venice

external viewing only

5E, 9S, 10S, 12L, 45, N2, ST1 > San Marco Sansovino
31H > Sansovino Vespucci

The INA-Casa Villaggio San Marco district, was designed by Giuseppe Samonà between 1950 and 1963 as part of a national public residential building plan, and represents a significant example of post-war experimental architecture in Venice. Located in an area of urban expansion on the Venetian mainland, the complex was designed as part of an urban project to provide working class homes, without forgetting attention to design and innovative style. Samonà designed the district according to a layout that included row housing and tower blocks, creating a dynamic composition that eliminated the severity of more orthodox Rationalist design. He used traditional materials like exposed brick and tiled roofing, combined with modern solutions that focused on functional space and a better life-style quality for the inhabitants. The housing was arranged around pedestrian walkways and planted green areas, designed to encourage social contact and improved liveability in neighbourhoods. Despite their plain simple design, the buildings include details that are linked with Venetian tradition, such as the inclusion of loggias and regular rows of windows. This project demonstrates Samonà's commitment to creating an architectural style able to combine innovation and historic continuity, establishing the basis for deeper reflection on the subject of social housing in Italy.

© Alessandro Zanchini

architects	type	construction
Giuseppe Samonà	residential	1950-1963

82. IUAV Construction Sciences Laboratory

Via Torino 153/A
30172 Venice

external viewing only

31H, 32H, 43 >
Torino Università

Designed by Francesco Venezia and completed in 2004, the IUAV Construction Sciences Laboratory represents an emblematic project, combining academic precision, functional efficiency and wonderful spatial poetics. The building sits in an industrial urban context in a dialogue with its historic memory expressed through the project design, with its very strict lines, but charged with meaning. The building is developed in a sequence of spaces in a straight line, designed as a physical and intellectual "route". The interior spaces, designed to house teaching laboratories and research areas, feature a well-balanced combination of solids and voids where natural light plays a fundamental role. Exposed concrete, brick and wood demonstrate the architect's research into material aspects, a core feature in Francesco Venezia's work: each surface, each constructive detail, becomes a reflection of the connection between function, materials and time. The external space was designed with a piazza for access, and an internal courtyard, recalling the traditional Venetian campiello, but in a more essential, contemporary interpretation. This type of approach is never designed merely for functional reasons, but is aimed at establishing an emotional communication with the context and the user, in which architecture provides a spatial and symbolic experience.

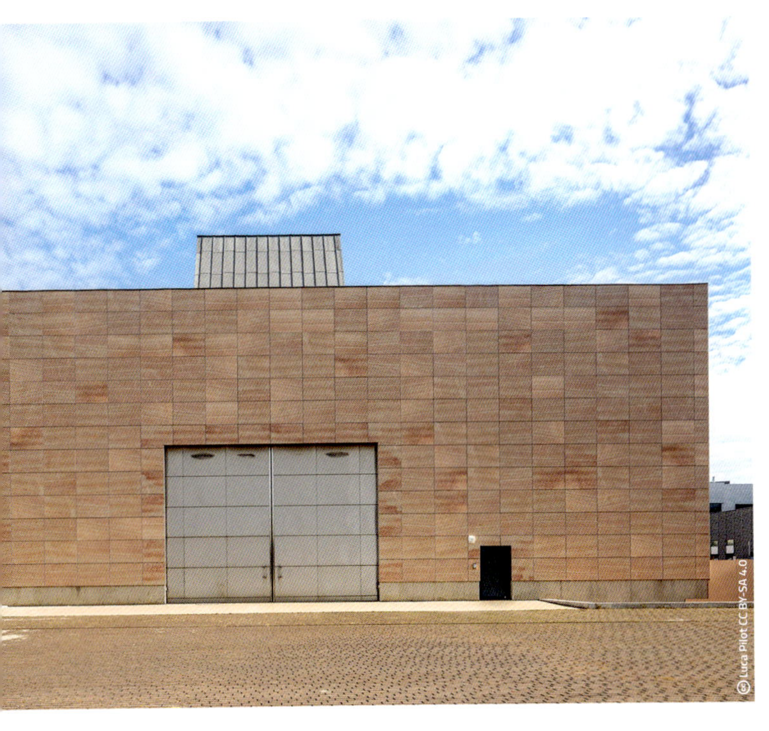

architects
Francesco Venezia

type
institutional

construction
2004

83. Aquae Pavilion

Via Galileo Ferraris 5
30175 Venice

external viewing only

Venezia Porto Marghera

2, 4, 4L, 6, 6L,7, 7E, 7L, 8, 8E, 12E, 25, 53E, 66, 66E, 81F, N1, PK1
> Via della Libertà
8, 25 > Mestre – Via Righi

The Aquae Pavilion, designed by AMDL CIRCLE and Michele De Lucchi, is an installation that provokes an evocative reflection on the relationship between the architecture, environment, and the fluctuating natural conditions in Venice. This temporary pavilion is part of the office's research into lightweight construction and the relationship between constructed space and the landscape, expressing these aspects in an intervention that communicates with the fluid, constantly changing character of the lagoon; in fact, the reversible modular structure is designed to adapt to the changes in water levels, highlighting the uncertainty and variability of the Venetian environment. The core element of the composition is a grid structure in laminated wood, supported by steel pillars anchored to floating platforms. The transparent shell provides complete visual permeability, erasing the distinction between interior and exterior, and creating a play of reflections where the structure seems to dissolve in the light and water. The use of plain simple materials is a nod to traditional Venetian construction. The internal layout is deliberately flexible, with mobile dividing panels that can transform the space according to different types of event or artistic installation. Aquae Pavilion is not only an example of temporary architecture, but also a manifesto to demonstrate architecture's capacity to adapt and integrate with the landscape in a respectful and sustainable manner. With this project, AMDL CIRCLE and De Lucchi offer a profound reflection on the fragility and beauty of Venice, demonstrating how architecture can express poetics able to benefit the constantly changing nature of Venice. The Pavilion is currently in a state of abandon. However even in this condition, a piece of architecture is never completely devoid of life: it is simply waiting to embrace a new function, ready to receive new narratives and new meanings.

© Alessandra Chemollo. Courtesy AMDL CIRCLE

architects
AMDL CIRCLE and
Michele De Lucchi

type
cultural

construction
2015

Museums

Museo Correr
Venetian art and history museum
-
P.za San Marco 52, 30124 Venice

correr.visitmuve.it
prenotazionivenezia@coopculture.it
Tel +39 041 2405211

Ca' Rezzonico
Museum of 18th century venetian art
-
Sestiere Dorsoduro 3136, 30123 Venice

carezzonico.visitmuve.it
prenotazionivenezia@coopculture.it
Tel +39 041 2410100

Ca' Pesaro
Gallery of international and modern art
-
Santa Croce, Calle del Tentor 2076, 30135 Venice

capesaro.visitmuve.it
prenotazionivenezia@coopculture.it
Tel +39 041 721127

Museo del Vetro
Museum of Murano glassware
-
Fondamenta Giustinian 8, 30141 Murano

museovetro.visitmuve.it
prenotazionivenezia@coopculture.it
Tel +39 041 2434914

Museo di Storia Naturale
Museum on fish and animals of the Venetian Lagoon
-
Salizada del Fontego dei Turchi 1730, 30135 Venice

msn.visitmuve.it
nat.mus.ve@fmcvenezia.it
Tel +39 041 2700303

Palazzo Mocenigo
Research centre: fabrics, costumes, and perfumes
-
Calle del Tentor 1992, 30135 Venice

mocenigo.visitmuve.it
mocenigo@fmcvenezia.it
Tel +39 041 721798

Museo Fortuny
Mariano Fortuny house museum
-
San Marco 3958, 30124 Venice

fortuny.visitmuve.it
fortuny@fmcvenezia.it
Tel +39 041 5200995

Museo del Merletto
Lace-making museum
-
Piazza Galuppi 187, 30142 Burano

museomerletto.visitmuve.it
museo.merletto@fmcvenezia.it
Tel +39 041 730034

Casa di Carlo Goldoni
Palazzo Centani house museum
-
San Polo 2794, 30125 Venice

carlogoldoni.visitmuve.it
segreteria.casagoldoni@fmcvenezia.it
Tel +39 041 2759325

Gallerie dell'Accademia di Venezia
Museum of Venetian and Veneto regional art
-
Campo della Carità, Dorsoduro 1050,
30123 Venice

www.gallerieaccademia.it
ga-ave@cultura.gov.it
Tel +39 041 5222247

Museo Storico Navale
Naval history museum
-
Riva S. Biasio 2148, 30122 Venice

munav.it
info@munav.it
Tel +39 041 5754259

Galleria Giorgio Franchetti alla Ca' d'Oro
Ancient art museum
-
Sestiere Cannaregio, 3932 Venice

www.cadoro.org
Tel +39 041 5222349

Museo d'Arte Orientale
Modern art museum
-
Ca' Pesaro, Sestiere di Santa Croce 2076, 30100 Venice

orientalevenezia.beniculturali.it
drm-ven.orientale@cultura.gov.it
Tel +39 041 5241173

Le Stanze del Vetro
Museum of 20th century and contemporary glassware
-
Isola di San Giorgio Maggiore 8, 30124 Venice

lestanzedelvetro.org
info@lestanzedelvetro.org
Tel +39 041 5229138

Museo Ebraico di Venezia
Museum of silverware and fabric furnishings of the Venetian Jewish community
-
Campo di Ghetto Nuovo 2902, 30121 Venice

www.ghettovenezia.com/museo
ghettovenezia@operalaboratori.com
Tel +39 041 5246083

Museo della Musica
Venetian musical history museum
-
S. Marco 2603, 30124 Venice

www.museodellamusica.com
info@museodellamusica.com
Tel +39 041 2411840

Scuola Grande San Giovanni Evangelista
Museum of gothic art and architecture
-
San Polo 2454, 30125 Venice

www.scuolasangiovanni.it
info@scuolasangiovanni.it
Tel +39 041 718234

Scuola Grande dei Carmini
Venetian cultural centre
-
Sestiere Dorsoduro 2617, 30123 Venice

www.scuolagrandecarmini.it
info@scuolagrandecarmini.it
Tel +39 041 5289420

Palazzo Vendramin Grimani
Contemporary art museum
-
San Polo 2033, 30125 Venice

www.fondazionealberodoro.org/it
info@fondazionealberodoro.org
Tel +39 041 8727750

Fondazione Giorgio e Armanda Marchesani
Art gallery and exhibition space
-
Sestiere Dorsoduro 2525, 30123 Venice

fondazionemarchesani.org
info@fondazionemarchesani.org
Tel +39 041 3084944

Theatres

Teatro La Fenice
Campo S. Fantin 1965, 30124 Venice
www.teatrolafenice.it
info@teatrolafenice.org
Tel +39 041 2722 699

Teatro Carlo Goldoni (Teatro Stabile Veneto)
S. Marco 4650/B, 30124 Venice
www.teatrostabileveneto.it
info@teatrostabileveneto.it
Tel +39 041 2402 011

Teatro Malibran
Campiello del Teatro 5873, 30133 Venice
www.teatrolafenice.it
info@teatrolafenice.org
Tel +39 041 2722 699

Ateneo di San Basso
P.za San Marco 315, 30124 Venice
www.musicinvenice.com
info@musicinvenice.com
Tel +39 348 1908 939

Teatro a l'Avogaria
Corte Zappa, Dorsoduro 1617, 30123 Venice
www.teatro-avogaria.it
avogaria@gmail.com
Tel +39 335 372 889

Teatro Fondamenta Nuove
Cannaregio 5013, 30121 Venice
www.teatrofondamentanuove.it
Tel +39 041 5220 044

Auditorium Lo Squero
Isola di San Giorgio, Venice
www.cini.it
info@cini.it
Tel +39 041 2710 202

Teatro Junghans
Giudecca 494/B, 30133 Venice
www.accademiateatraleveneta.com/teatro-junghans
Tel +39 041 2411 974

Teatrino Groggia
Cannaregio 3150, 30121 Venice
www.piccionaia.org/teatrinogroggia/
apescadisogni@piccionaia.org
Tel +39 041 5244 665

Teatro Toniolo
Piazzetta Gian Francesco Malipiero 1,
30174 Venice
www.comune.venezia.it/content/teatro-toniolo
Tel +39 349 7723 552

Teatro Ca' Foscari
Calle Larga S. Marta 2137, 30121 Venice
www.unive.it
Tel +39 041 2348 962

Teatro Piccolo Arsenale – Biennale di Venezia
Campo de la Tana 2161, 30122 Venice
www.labiennale.org
info@labiennale.org
Tel +39 041 5218 711

Teatro alle Tese – Biennale di Venezia
Calle Larga Rosa 77, 30122 Venice
www.labiennale.org
info@labiennale.org
Tel +39 041 5218 711

Hotels

• • • expensive
• • mid-range
• inexpensive

B&B Corte dei Miracoli •
Calle Moretti 5508, 30121 Venice
Tel +39 334 8390 715

Belmond Hotel Cipriani • • •
Giudecca 10, 30133 Venice
www.belmond.com
Tel +39 041 240 801

Ca Nigra Lagoon Resort • • •
Campiello S. Simeone Grande 927, 30135 Venice
www.hotelcanigra.com
info@hotelcanigra.com
Tel +39 041 2750 047

Hilton Molino Stucky Venice • • •
Giudecca 810, 30133 Venice
molinostuckyhilton.it
info@hilton.com
Tel +39 041 2723 311

Hotel Alcyone • •
Calle dei Fabbri 4712, 30124 Venice
www.hotelalcyonevenice.com
info@hotelalcyone.com
Tel +39 041 5212 508

Hotel Campiello •
Calle del Vin 4647, 30122 Venice
www.hcampiello.it
campiello@hotelcampiello.com
Tel +39 041 5205 764

Hotel Canal Grande • •
Campiello S. Simeone Grande 932, 30135 Venice
www.hotelcanalgrande.it
info@hotelcanalgrande.it
Tel +39 041 2440 148

Hotel Giudecca • •
Calle Ferrando 409, 30133 Venice
www.hotelgiudeccavenezia.it
giudecca@primahotel.it
Tel +39 041 2960 168

Hotel Indigo Venice • •
Calle Buccari 10, 30132 Sant'Elena, Venice
www.indigovenice.com
info@indigovenice.com
Tel +39 041 2717 811

Hotel Nani Mocenigo Palace • • •
Fondamenta Nani, 960, 30123 Venice
www.hotelnanimocenigo.com
info@hotelnanimocenigo.com
Tel +39 041 5200 145

Hotel Pausania • •
Fondamenta Gherardini 2824, 30123 Venice
www.hotelpausania.it
info@hotelpausania.it
Tel +39 041 5222 083

Hotel Santa Chiara • •
Santa Croce 548, 30135 Venice
www.hotelsantachiara.it
info@hotelsantachiara.it
Tel +39 041 5228 799

Hotel Santo Stefano • •
Campo Santo Stefano 2957, 30124 Venice
hotelsantostefanovenezia.com
info@hotelsantostefanove
Tel +39 041 5200 166

Ostello Domus Civica •
Sestiere San Polo 3082, (Calle de le Sechere), 30125 Venice
www.domuscivica.com
info@domuscivica.com
Tel +39 041 721 103

The St. Regis Venice • • •
P.za San Marco 2159, 30124 Venice
www.marriott.com
venice.butler@stregis.com
Tel +39 041 2400 001

Restaurants

• • • expensive
• • mid-range
• inexpensive

Ae Oche San Giacomo •
Ramo Quinto Gallion O del Pezzetto 1552/A, 30135 Venice
Tel +39 041 7178 79

Ai Do Leoni •
P.za San Marco 355, 30124 Venice
www.aidoleoni.com
aidoleonivenezia@gmail.com

Ai Mercanti • •
Corte Coppo 4346/A, 30124 Venice
aimercanti.it
info_aimercanti@libero.it
Tel +39 041 5238 269

Al Covo • • •
Campiello de la Pescaria 3968, 30122 Venice
ristorantealcovo.com
info@ristorantealcovo.com
Tel +39 041 5223 812

Al Profeta •
C. Lunga S. Barnaba 2671, 30123 Venice
alprofeta.it
info@alprofeta.it
Tel +39 041 5237 466

Bacaro Quebrado •
Calle Larga dei Bari 1107/A, 30121 Venice
Tel +39 041 5280 977

Canova by Sadler • • •
P.za San Marco 1243, 30124 Venice
canovarestaurant.com
sadler@sadler.it
Tel +39 041 8040 062

Chat Qui Rit • • •
Calle Tron 1131, 30124 Venice
chatquirit.it
chatquirit@chatquirit.it
Tel +39 041 5229 086

Oro Restaurant • • •
Giudecca 10, 30133 Venice
www.belmond.com
ororestaurant.cip@belmond.com
Tel +39 041 240 801

Osteria Al Squero •
Dorsoduro 943, 30123 Venice
Tel +39 041 2960 479

Osteria Da Codroma • •
Fondamenta Briati 2540, 30123 Venice
codroma@yahoo.it
Tel +39 041 5246 789

Osteria Enoteca Ai Artisti • •
Fondamenta Toletta 1169/ABC, 30123 Venice
www.enotecaartisti.com
info@enotecaartisti.com
Tel +39 041 5238 944

Osteria La Zucca • •
Sestiere Santa Croce 1762, 30135 Venice
www.lazucca.it
Tel +39 041 5241 570

Quadri • • •
P.za San Marco, 30124 Venice
alajmo.it/pages/homepage-ristorante-quadri
booking@alajmo.it
Tel +39 041 5222 105

Trattoria Dai Tosi •
Castello 738, 30122 Venice
www.trattoriadaitosi.it
Tel +39 041 5237 102

Architectural offices

120 grammi :: laboratorio di architettura
Via delle Industrie 15, 30175 Marghera, Venice
www.120lab.net
studio@120lab.net
Tel +39 347 5891125

_apml | Architetti Pedron / La Tegola
Santa Croce 1327, 30135 Venice
www.apml-architetti.it
info@apml-architetti.it
Tel +39 041 8779166

Bisà
Burano Island, San Martino Sinistro 872, 30142 Venice
Via Rampa Cavalcavia 1, 30172 Venice
www.bisa.eu
info@bisa.eu
Tel +39 041 735032
Tel +39 041 4768200

Cecchetto & Associati
Via Torino 107, 30172 Venice
www.cecchettoassociati.com
studio@studiocecchetto.com
Tel +39 041 5240440

cfk architetti
San Polo 2702/A, 30125 Venice
www.cfk.it
cfk@cfk.it
Tel +39 041 2750019

Enrico Dusi Studio
San Polo 3083, 30125 Venice
www.enricodusi.com
mail@enricodusi.com

Giorgio Pettenò Architetti
Fondamenta dei Cereri 2425 A, 30123 Venice
www.giorgiopetteno.com
studio@giorgiopetteno.com
Tel +39 041 714532

H&A Associati
Via Banchina dell'Azoto 15/d, 30175 Venice
www.hastudio.it
info@hastudio.it
Tel +39 041 922888

KANZ Architetti
Calle Lunga San Barnaba 2858, 30123 Venice
www.kanzarchitetti.com
info@kanzarchitetti.com
Tel +39 041 528 4291

MAP studio
Dorsoduro 3464, 30123 Venice
www.map-studio.it
info@map-studio.it
Tel +39 041 720979

Mide Architetti
Via Barbariga 47/B, 30032 Fiesso d'Artico, Venice
www.midearchitetti.it
info@midearchitetti.it
Tel +39 049 645 9020

Studio architetti Mar
Via Castellana 60, 30174 Venice
www.studioarchitettimar.eu
mar@studioarchitettimar.eu
Tel +39 041 984477

Studio Zordan
Sestiere Dorsoduro 3082, 30123 Venice
www.zordan.asia
studio@studiozordan.it
Tel +39 041 5242866

TAMassociati
Sestiere Dorsoduro 2731, 30123 Venice
www.tamassociati.org
info@tamassociati.org
Tel +39 041 5226974

Index by architect

Index by project

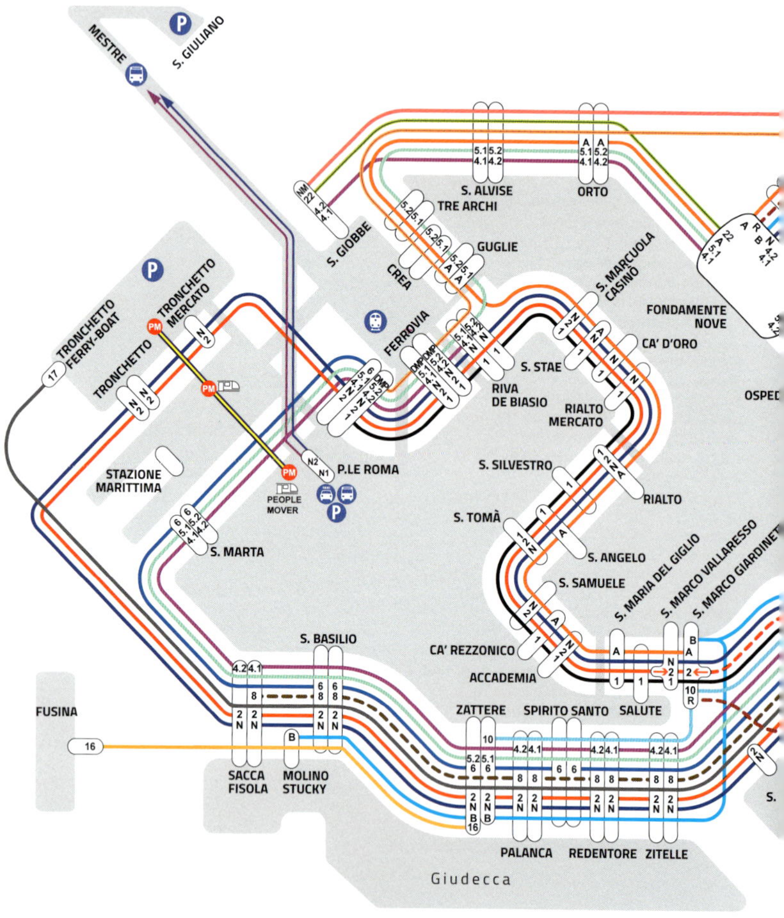

MESTRE
S. GIULIANO
S. GIOBBE
S. ALVISE
ORTO
TRE ARCHI
GUGLIE
CREA
TRONCHETTO FERRY-BOAT
TRONCHETTO MERCATO
TRONCHETTO
FERROVIA
S. MARCUOLA CASINÒ
FONDAMENTE NOVE
CA' D'ORO
S. STAE
RIVA DE BIASIO
RIALTO MERCATO
OSPED
STAZIONE MARITTIMA
PEOPLE MOVER
P.LE ROMA
S. SILVESTRO
RIALTO
S. TOMÀ
S. MARTA
S. ANGELO
S. SAMUELE
S. MARIA DEL GIGLIO
S. MARCO VALLARESSO
S. MARCO GIARDINET
S. BASILIO
CA' REZZONICO
ACCADEMIA
FUSINA
ZATTERE
SPIRITO SANTO
SALUTE
SACCA FISOLA
MOLINO STUCKY
PALANCA
REDENTORE
ZITELLE
S.
Giudecca

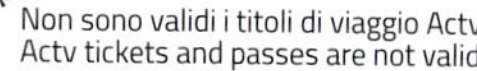
* Non sono validi i titoli di viaggio Actv
Actv tickets and passes are not valid

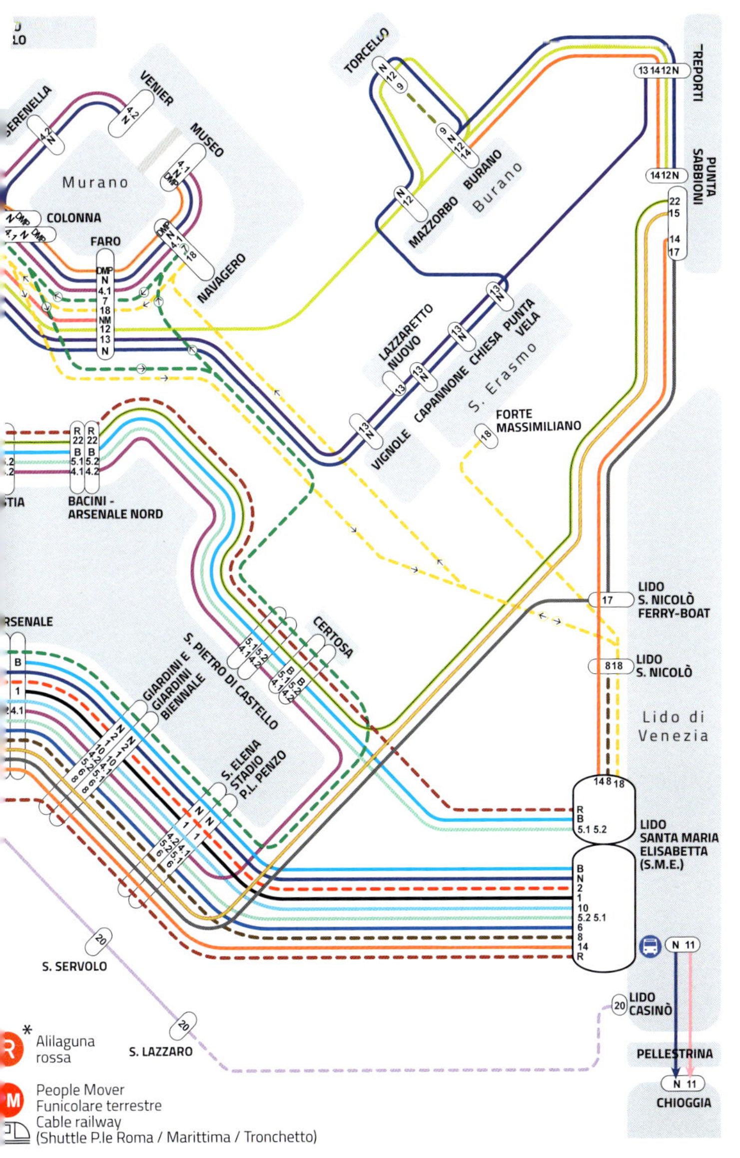

Murano
SERENELLA
VENIER
MUSEO
COLONNA
FARO
NAVAGERO
TORCELLO
BURANO
Burano
MAZZORBO
TREPORTI
PUNTA SABBIONI
LAZZARETTO NUOVO
CAPANNONE
CHIESA
PUNTA VELA
S. Erasmo
VIGNOLE
FORTE MASSIMILIANO
BACINI - ARSENALE NORD
CERTOSA
S. PIETRO DI CASTELLO
GIARDINI E GIARDINI BIENNALE
S. ELENA STADIO P.L. PENZO
LIDO S. NICOLÒ FERRY-BOAT
LIDO S. NICOLÒ
Lido di Venezia
LIDO SANTA MARIA ELISABETTA (S.M.E.)
LIDO CASINÒ
S. SERVOLO
S. LAZZARO
PELLESTRINA
CHIOGGIA
Alilaguna rossa
People Mover
Funicolare terrestre
Cable railway
(Shuttle P.le Roma / Marittima / Tronchetto)

This volume was printed in July 2025
by ABC Tipografia, Calenzano, Florence